COMMUNITY AWARD SCHEMES

A Guide to National and Local Award Schemes and Competitions with Cash Prizes

by Stephen Woollett

published by the Directory of Social Change

COMMUNITY AWARD SCHEMES

by Stephen Woollett

cover design Beverly Tattersfield

First published in this form 1990
Published by the Directory of Social Change
© Directory of Social Change, 1990

Typeset by Kerry Robinson
Printed in Britain by Biddles of Guildford

No part of this publication may be reproduced in any form whatsoever without prior permission in writing from the publishers.

ISBN 0 907164 56 0

Directory of Social Change, Radius Works, Back Lane, London NW3 1HL

CONTENTS

Introduction 1
Award schemes listed alphabetically 9
Index by subject category with
   geographical eligibility 163

Alphabetical listing of schemes covered in this book

ABSA/Daily Telegraph Awards	9
AFASIC Christmas Card Competition	10
Art and Work Awards	11
Arts in the Community Awards	12
Association for Industrial Archaeology Awards	14
Association for the Protection of Rural Scotland (APRS) Awards	16
The Augustine Courtauld Award	17
Barclays Youth Action	18
BBC Girl of the Year	19
BBC Design Awards	20
Best Kept Village Competitions	22
Best of British Youth Awards	26
Best Social Inventions Prize	27
BET Choristers Award	28
Brecknock Community Environmental Project Competiton	30
Britain in Bloom	31
The Business and Industry Environment Awards	33
Caring in the Community	34
Charity Annual Report and Accounts Award	35
Child of Achievement Awards	36
Civic/Architectural Design Awards	37
The Colonel Sanders Environmental Awards	39
Community Care Enterprise Awards	40
Community Partnership Prize	42
Community Planning Awards	43
Communty Pride Awards	44
Co-Operative Community Awards Scheme	46
Countryside Caretakers Award	47
Country Life Farming and Wildlife Award	48
The Daily Telegraph Award	49
The Daily Telegraph School Newspaper Competition	50
The Dista Awards for Young People with Arthritis	51
Domestic Health Education Awards	52
The Dragon Awards	54
Duchy of Cornwall Devon Young Farmers Clubs Countryside Proj.	55
Dulux Community Projects	57
(County) Durham Environment Award	58
ETHA - Education Through Heritage and the Arts	59
Edward Morshead Award	60
Elmbridge Community Clean Up Prize	61
Environmental Enterprise Award	62
Environment Week Awards	64
Ethnic Minorities Award Scheme (EMAS)	65
Europa Nostra Awards	66
Eyebright	68
Eyebright Junior	69
Ford Conservation Awards	70
Gateway Interpret Britain Award	72
The Glenfiddich Living Scotland Award	74
Gloucestershire Footpath Heritage Competition	75
The Graham Allen Award for Conservation	76
Great Envelope Competition	77
Green Con of the Year Award	78
Green Leaf Housing Awards	80
Gulbenkian Museum and Galleries Awards	81
Habitat Awards	82

The Ian Allan Railway Heritage Awards	84
Ideas Annual Competition	85
The Independent Living Awards	86
It's My City	87
The Jaap Joustra Award for Outstanding Achievement	89
The John Hunt Awards	90
The John Mejor Award	92
Lincoln Civic Award	93
Literary Awards	94
Livewire	95
Mayor of Bournemouth Volunteer of the Year Award	96
Mersey Basin Campaign Awards	97
Midlands Women of the Year Awards	98
Museum of the Year Awards	99
Museums Year Award	101
NFCO Publicity Competition	102
The Norfold Society Awards	103
North York Moors National Park Conservation Awards	104
Nothumberland Tree and Hedgerow Cup Competition	105
Pride of Place Awards	106
The Prince of Wales Award	107
Prudential Awards for the Arts	108
Ratcliff Mobility Award	110
Reform 'Compassionate Action' Trust Award	111
RICS Conservation Awards	112
The Right Livelihood Awards	113
Royal Insurance Young Critic Award	114
The Royal Mail Sports Club Award Scheme	115
Royal Mail Young Letter-Writers Competition	116
RTPI Annual Award for Planning Achievement	118
RSPB Birds and Countryside Awards	120
Rural Employment Award	121
Rural Wales Awards	122
Sainsbury's Choir of the Year Competition	123
The Sandford Award	124
Scania Transport Trust Awards	126
Scottish Museum of the Year Awards	127
Scottish Playgrounds of the Year Awards	128
Scottish Tourism Award	130
Shell Better Britain Campaign	131
South Somerset Environmental Awards Scheme	133
Steam Heritage Awards	134
Theakston Heritage Fund	135
The Community Chest	137
Times/PM Environment Award	138
The Times/RIBA Community Enterprise Scheme	139
Tomorrow's New Communities Competition	141
Trees for People: Arboretum Competition	143
T.S. Shipman Prize	144
TSW Shootfirst Award	144
Tunstall Telecom National Caring Awards	146
TV-AM Caring Christmas Schools Competition	147
Twin Town Awards	148
Village Hall Awards	149
Village Ventures	150
VPB Design Award for Interpretive Panels	154
Wainwright Achievement Award	155
Whitbread Volunteer Action Awards	156
Wimpy Environmental Awards with UK 2000	157
Wimpy Walks Awards	158
Young Concert Artists' Award	159
Yong Deaf Achievers Award	160
Youth Clubs of the Year	160

Acknowledgements

Grateful thanks are due to all those who responded to our initial request for information and to our subsequent queries and questions. Special thanks to Neil Irving of East Yorkshire CVS who identified twenty four schemes for us to research.

Thanks should also go to Saskia Hallam, Jacynth Black, Juliette Fleming and Doreen Piano and most especially to Helen Strivens whose assistance with the research for this book was invaluable.

Introduction

This Guide contains information on over 120 competitions and award schemes throughout the United Kingdom which have a 'community' dimension. Awards for individuals and in other fields are not covered. The majority of the schemes operate at a national level; some however have a quite local focus, a town, district or county for example; and a small number are European-wide or international schemes.

There is of course no hard and fast definition of what constitutes a competition or award scheme, but we have adopted the following broad criteria as the basis for inclusion in this book:

• Competitions should be open to charities, voluntary and community groups, schools or other non-profit making organisations. Competitions targeted at individuals or commercial businesses are included where the activities promoted and/or the awards themselves offer potential benefits to voluntary organisations or the community as a whole. An example is the *Business and Industry Environment Awards* which promote activities by companies to improve the environment. Another is the *Green Leaf Awards* for environmentally sensitive new housing schemes – here the prizes, of £1000 each, must be donated to a charity of the recipient's choice.

• In general we have included schemes which award projects and activities already completed, and thus recognise achievement, and have excluded schemes which give awards for plans and proposals. There are however a few exceptions, in particular where a scheme in the latter category is clearly promoted as a 'Competition'. Examples are the *Best Social Inventions Prize* and *Tomorrow's New Communities Award*.

• When in doubt about whether to include a particular scheme or not, perhaps because it operates more like a grant-making trust than a competition, we have tended towards inclusion, especially if information on the scheme is not readily available elsewhere. An example is the *Barclays Youth Action* scheme.

Why the book has been produced

There were two main reasons why we felt that this Guide would be a valuable addition to our existing range of publications. Firstly it was clear that competitions can generate considerable publicity for award winning projects and organisations. High profile presentation ceremonies, press articles and media attention may be extremely valuable. The awards themselves, usually cash and/or some other sort of prize, may be less significant although obviously welcome. We estimate that the total value of the cash prizes offered through schemes listed in this Guide amounts to over £1 million per year, although over half this sum (about 52%) is generated by just seven of the schemes.

The second reason why we have published this Guide is to assist competition organisers and their sponsors. There seems to have been a proliferation of schemes over the past few years as commercial sponsors and their public relations agencies have jumped at the chance of gaining substantial publicity allied to support for a 'worthy cause'. Some have succeeded and some have not. Inevitably there has been some duplication and wasted effort. So it seemed sensible to produce this Guide as a resource for those considering establishing new schemes or adapting existing ones. Perhaps it might also encourage a little more cross-fertilisation of ideas and experience between competition organisers.

How the book is organised

Each competition or award scheme we have been able to identify has an entry in the Guide and these are ordered alphabetically. The index at the end of the book lists the schemes in thirteen categories according to the type of activities/projects/organisations eligible to enter and also indicates the geographical criterion for eligibility. Inevitably these categories are simplified and cannot adequately reflect the particular and sometimes quite detailed criteria for individual schemes. So we suggest that if you are interested in identifying specific types of scheme, perhaps those which your own organisation might be eligible to enter, that you look through all the entries in the book.

We have not always been able to confirm whether a competition will be continuing in future years, or if it is, whether eligibility criteria, prizes and awards and the organisation of the scheme will remain the same. You should therefore seek up to date information directly from the contacts listed. In almost all cases the organisers publish information leaflets and other material about their scheme and these are commonly updated each year.

How the information was collected

We identified schemes for possible inclusion in this Guide by requesting information from all local authorities (except parish councils), several hundred national and local voluntary organisations (through the National Council for Voluntary Organisations and the equivalent bodies in Scotland and Wales) and over fifty specialist agencies and intermediary bodies. We also culled annual reports and other information from the major corporate donors and trawled a variety of magazines, journals and newspapers. In spite of what we feel was a fairly comprehensive search, we are certain to have excluded some schemes. For any omissions we apologise – but please send us information on any schemes we have missed.

The research for this Guide provides a salutary lesson to competition organisers. It proved remarkably difficult to obtain information on many schemes, including some which appear to seek a high publicity profile. Many times our telephone calls were transferred from person to person, none of whom could supply even basic information. It is easy to imagine potential entrants put off by such a response.

Advice to entrants

The following advice is based on the comments of a number of people directly involved in organising competitions:

1. While some competitions may attract several hundred and even thousands of entries, there are those that receive remarkably few. So do seriously consider entering – if you do enter, your chances of winning an award may be quite good.

2. In spite of the advice above, do not be too hasty. It may be better to delay your application until you really have got a tangible achievement under your belt – especially if you are confident that the competition will be continuing in future years.

3. Some competitions which are geared primarily to individuals can also benefit organisations with which the person is involved. Perhaps

there are people supporting your organisation worthy of nomination. *The Whitbread Community Care Award* is an example.

4. There is no reason why you should not enter a project, or different aspects of it, in more than one competition.

5. Remember that the prestige and publicity which can come with an award may be extremely valuable. So do not think of the competition purely in terms of the cash value of awards.

6. Many schemes welcome and some require 'before and after' photographs to assist judges and for use by the media. Try to keep some photographic record of your project even if you are not currently considering entering a scheme.

7. How you present your application is particularly important. In the words of one competition organiser – 'Stop and think'. Think through carefully what you want to say and prepare a rough draft of your application which you can refine – perhaps with the help of others. If there is an application form complete this fully and clearly. If at all possible, type it – remember it will almost certainly be photocopied and passed to a judging panel. Unless specifically disallowed, include as much background information, press cuttings, photographs and other material as you think appropriate. The initial judging may well be based solely on submissions.

8. If you do win an award, then make the most of it in terms of publicity. Your local media are virtually certain to cover a project 'on their patch' which has gained an award at national or regional level. It should also impress your sponsors and supporters too – it may be a good opportunity to bring them together to say 'thank you'.

Advice to organisers

This advice is inevitably of a general nature – much will depend on your aims and objectives, geographical coverage and so on.

1. Research other competitions (using this book!) to ensure that you do not duplicate or compete with existing schemes. You should also be able to get useful advice from other competition organisers.

2. Do not underestimate the cost of organising a competition. For some competitions the value of prizes and awards is only a small proportion of the total cost of managing and promoting the scheme. (This perhaps begs the question: Who benefits most – the activities or organisations promoted or the PR agency which runs the scheme?) If successful your competition will probably attract an increasing

number of entries (and inquiries) which will mean more administrative work. One major award scheme has recently appointed a full-time coordinator.

3. You may wish to consider tapping into an existing competition rather than setting up a new one. For example *The Times/RIBA Community Enterprise* scheme has included specific awards sponsored by the Community Projects Foundation, and the National Childrens Play and Recreation Unit. The experience of one scheme coordinator suggests that one central coordinating/contact point for entries is virtually essential.

4. It clearly helps in attracting publicity if you have one or two well known people to help promote the scheme, head the judging team, or present the awards. This may be especially important for commercial sponsors in terms of the publicity spin-offs.

5. There are various schools of thought on the size and nature of awards. Some feel that a small number of relatively large cash awards is more effective at generating entries than several smaller awards while others feel the reverse. In some competitions the prestige of winning, recognised perhaps only by a plaque, is all that seems to matter. Its probably simply a question of horses for courses. However, especially if you are starting a new competition, it is worth considering not specifying exactly what prizes are on offer or at least to hold back a certain amount to be used at the judges discretion.

6. Do not underestimate the time you need to allow between launching a scheme and the deadline for entries. Disseminating information through the networks of the voluntary sector can be a long process. Decisions on whether or not to enter may need to wait until the 'next committee meeting'.

7. Consider the appropriateness of offering grants for proposed projects, perhaps as well as awards for achievement, and ways of promoting the examples of good practice which the scheme generates.

Types of schemes

An analysis of the schemes by subject category (as used in the index) reveals the following:

Arts	10
Business/industry	4
Community action	11
Community care/social welfare	5

Disability/health	7
Education/schools	8
Environment	44
Housing/planning	6
Individual achievement	13
Museums/heritage/archaeology	16
Tourism/recreation	3
Voluntary sector – general	10
Youth	3

[The total is more than the number of schemes in this book because some fall into more than one category. Where a similar scheme is organised in several different geographical areas (such as the county *Village Ventures* or *Best Kept Village Competitions*) then these are recorded only once.]

The analysis above shows that the environment is by far the most popular single theme for competitions with 31% of schemes. Museum/heritage interpretation/archaeological schemes rank second with 11%. This is not surprising because these types of project are tangible and relatively easily judged and provide good visual material for publicity conscious sponsors. Given the increasing awareness of environmental issues amongst the public, the media, business and government, it seems unlikely that the environment will become less popular as a theme for competitions. Probably the reverse.

Why competitions?

Most competitions in the field of social and community action are designed, at least in part, to promote and encourage good practice.

They can be an effective means of identifying and bringing to public attention, or the attention of a particular network, projects and activities which can be held up as examples of excellence. Thus they are, by and large, a means to an end rather than an end in themselves. Thus the Society for the Interpretation of Britain's Heritage annual *Gateway Interpret Britain Awards* provides an effective means of promoting a high standard of environmental and heritage interpretation. Award winners put on an exhibition at the presentation ceremony and their projects are written up into a loose leaf 'Manual of Good Practice'. Many of the Rural Community Councils which organise *Village Venture Competitions* for rural community projects publish reports on the winning projects to encourage and stimulate others.

The majority of competitions, at least at national level, depend heavily on some form of commercial sponsorship, but many are organised directly by companies or their agencies – for example, the *Whitbread Community Care Awards*, the *Sainsbury Choir of the Year Competition* and *The Times/PM Environment Awards*. For such companies, competitions provide valuable opportunities for straightforward publicity and an effective vehicle for promoting their corporate responsibility image. Whitbread regards its now well established Community Care Awards as the 'flagship of the company's extensive community involvement programme '. The Prince of Wales' patronage of the Community Enterprise Scheme organised by RIBA clearly brings prestige and no doubt some extra advertising revenue to the scheme's major sponsor – The Times newspaper.

Competitions and award schemes are not, and never can be, a substantial or secure source of funding for voluntary organisations.

Indeed it must be rather disillusioning to some organisations and individuals to see the sums of money lavished by commercial sponsors on 'glittering and prestigous' award ceremonies, on glossy publications and high profile media advertising, when the (small number of) winners receive relatively little. It is disappointing too that so few scheme organisers or sponsors appear to put much effort into disseminating the experience and 'good practice' of their entrants in general, and winners in particular. Some honourable exceptions are *Its My City* (which published a fascinating directory of over 700 entrants), and the *Shell Better Britain Campaign* (which produces a listing of all projects which receive a grant from the Campaign).

There are probably few cases where the existence of a competition and thus the chance of winning an award in itself stimulates activity. In most cases the timescale will be too tight and there will be other far more important factors affecting a project's viability. *Best Kept Village* and other local environmentally orientated competitions are probably the main exceptions.

The future

Amidst the proliferation of competitions and awards in virtually every area of charitable and voluntary activity, there is some evidence to suggest that voluntary organisations and commercial sponsors are beginning to recognise that more grant-orientated schemes, which help new projects to get off the ground, rather than awards which recognise achievement, may be a more constructive approach.

The *Shell Better Britain Campaign*, which has evolved out of a competition, but which now concentrates on the provision of grants, advice and information, the *Civic Trust/British Telecom Community Pride Awards*, the *Ethnic Minorities Award Scheme*, and the *Community Care Enterprise Awards* are good examples. In these sorts of schemes the money is directed at the groups and projects that really need it, rather than those that have already been successful.

There seems to be no reason why grant-based schemes should not generate the same level of publicity (for sponsors and organisers) as the more usual competitive awards. Indeed some schemes incorporate both – projects in receipt of grants are eligible at a later stage for awards based on their achievements. (*Dulux Community Projects* which selects for special cash awards particularly meritorious projects from among those which have received free paint under the scheme is an example.) The presentation of a substantial grant cheque can be just as newsworthy as the presentation of an award. Grant-based schemes can also include ways of disseminating examples of good practice and promoting high standards – for example through publications, training courses and seminars. An example is the *Environmental Enterprise Awards* run by WWF-UK where the awards themselves constitute just over 10% of the value of a £120,000 training and development programme.

An attractive feature of some, but not all, grant-based schemes is the flexibility of timing. Most competitions have a single annual deadline for submission of entries, while many of the schemes providing grants will accept applications at three or four points during the year. *Barclays Youth Action* has three deadlines for applications – in March, June and September; the *Glenfiddich Living Scotland Award* scheme accepts applications at any time.

We have not been able to estimate the total value of the cash and staff resources devoted to organising and promoting competitions and award schemes, but it is probably safe to assume that it is many times the direct value of the awards themselves (just over £1 million). Include the time and cost of preparing (often unsuccessful) applications by several thousand individuals and organisations each year and it is easy to feel that there is scope for some re-thinking by organisers and sponsors. Perhaps this book will give a little encouragement for this process to take place.

ABSA/DAILY TELEGRAPH AWARDS

The Annual Award Scheme for Business Sponsorship of the Arts

Association for Business Sponsorship of the Arts, Nutmeg House, 60 Gainsford Street, Butlers Wharf, London SE1 2NY
Telephone: 071 378 8143

Contact: Jane Leslie, Awards Administrator
Sponsor: Daily Telegraph

The ABSA/Daily Telegraph Awards for Business Sponsors of the Arts, in their 12th year [in 1989], are designed to 'recognise and encourage imaginative and effective sponsorship of the arts by commercial organisations in the United Kingdom'.

There are twelve awards made to businesses involved in arts sponsorship in the following categories: Corporate Programme, Single Project, First Time Sponsor, Youth Sponsorship, Commission of New Art in any Medium, Sponsorship of Art and Disabled People and Sponsorship of British Art Overseas. There is a special award, sponsored by BP for 'the arts organisation which has made the most effective use of sponsorship'. In 1989 this award was worth £3000.

Nominations are assessed by an independent panel of judges which in 1989 included Lady Harlech, Jennifer d'Abo, Tim Bell, Baroness Blackstone, Brenda Dean, P D James, and Nicholas Serota. ABSA states that judges '.... will evaluate the success of each sponsorship in achieving the objectives of the sponsor and will consider the value to the organisation being sponsored, irrespective of the sums of money spent or available. Geographical location, art form, access for disabled people, the size of the sponsoring company and the innovative nature of the sponsorship will be taken into account by the judges when making their final decision'.

While these Awards, which take the form of a £5000 cash prize, are (with the exception of the ABSA/BP Arts Award) for the sponsoring businesses, the publicity associated with them should be of considerable value to the sponsored organisations and projects.

The 1989 Awards were launched in May, with a closing date for nominations in September and a presentation ceremony in December.

Future: These Awards are now well established and are an important part of ABSA's work to promote business sponsorship of the arts. They look certain to continue for the foreseeable future.

Entry: Nominations must be made on the official form and signed on behalf of the sponsor and the sponsored. A further four typed A4 pages plus other material may be submitted.

Note 1: In 1989 a new award, The Daily Telegraph Award, was intoduced for the 'individual who has contributed most to the artistic success of a sponsored activity'. This is administered separately from the overall awards described above and has a separate entry in this book.

Note 2: ABSA administers the Business Sponsorship Incentive Scheme. The scheme provides government money to 'match' new business money applied to arts sponsorship. First time sponsorship from a business which has never sponsored the arts before may be matched £1 for £1 and additional sponsorship from a previous arts sponsor may be matched £1 for £3. The publicity leaflet for BSIS refers to 'awards' and 'commemorative certificates' which are presented to all sponsors. But they should not be confused with the ABSA/Daily Telegraph Awards outlined above. Further information on the BSIS can be obtained from the ABSA Head Office, address above, their Scottish Office (Room 613, West Port House, 102 West Port, Edinburgh, EH3 9HS, Tel: 031 228 4262) or their Welsh Office (9 Museum Place, Cardiff CF1 3NX, Tel: 0222 394717).

AFASIC CHRISTMAS CARD COMPETITION

Association For All Speech Impaired Children (AFASIC), 347 Central Markets, Smithfield, London EC1A 9NH

Telephone: 071 236 3632/6487

Contact: Janet Hackwood, Information and Liaison Officer

This competition is for the design of a Christmas card which will be reproduced and sold in aid of AFASIC. It is open to children under 16 years of age in Special Schools and Language Units in the United Kingdom. The competition, designed to generate publicity for AFASIC, and present a challenge to children with speech difficulties, has been run annually since 1983. Prizes, donated by firms, go the winner and several runners-up. The winner has the pleasure of seeing his/her design in print.

Rules for the 1990 competition are as follows:
- Designs in two colours only – one of which must be red.
- On good quality white paper.
- Designs need not be Christmas card size.
- Theme must be Christmas – boldly and simply drawn.
- Each child may submit up to three entries. (Send SAE for return of entries.)
- Drawings must have name, age and address on reverse.

The closing date for the 1990 competition is 1st March 1990.

Future: We assume the competition will continue in future.

Entry: Entries to be submitted according to the rules above to the AFASIC Central Office (address above).

ART AND WORK AWARDS

The Wapping Arts Trust, 15 Dock Street, London E1 8JL
Telephone: 071 481 1337

Contact: Dale Whatley/Amanda Basker
Sponsors: Capital and Counties plc, Segwick Group plc, Art for Offices Ltd. Organised in association with The Institute of Directors.

This scheme aims to encourage and reward the incorporation of art into working environments. Any project involving art in a commercial environment in the United Kingdom is eligible. Entries may be submitted from companies in all areas of business, industry and commerce in the public and private sectors and by property developers, architects, designers, arts associations, art galleries and artists. Only UK projects are eligible. There are three main awards:

1. An art collection for a corporate building – which may be a new or an on-going collection.

2. A work of art commissioned for a specific site for a corporate building.

3. The most outstanding contribution made to art in the working environment by a company, an architectural/design practice or an individual.

In each category the company in whose premises the winning entry is sited will receive a specially designed sculpture. The artist most closely associated with the winning site-specific commission (category 2), or the winner in category 3, will receive £1000.

Winners in 1988 included William Pye's water sculptures in Gatwick Airport's North Terminal and the contemporary art collection in the office of Central Selling Organisation. Judging involves an initial assessment of submissions followed by visits to shortlisted schemes. The judges (in 1989) were Sir Peter Wakefield (Director of the National Art-Collections Fund), Michael Manser (past President of RIBA) and Roger de Grey (President of the Royal Academy of Arts).

In 1989 entries had to be submitted by 8th September and awards were presented in London in November.

Future: We assume this scheme will continue.

Entry: On the official entry form with up to 24 colour slides (category 2) or 36 colour slides (category 1 and 3) and a written description of the project of up to three typed A4 pages. Supporting material such as brochures, photographs and catalogues may also be submitted.

ARTS IN THE COMMUNITY AWARDS

Arts Development Association, The Arts Centre, Vane Terrace, Darlington, County Durham, DL3 7AX

Telephone: 0325 465930

Contact: Rick Welton, Director
Sponsor: English Estates

The Arts in the Community Awards, which were launched in Autumn 1989, are designed 'specifically to benefit small arts projects which rarely receive business sponsorship'. The Awards are intended to 'encourage innovation, improve access and increase participation in the arts'. The scheme can be regarded as source of grant-aid, rather than prizes, in that the value of the awards relates to the needs of the applicants.

The scheme is open to any organisation which is an independent 'not-for-profit' body, had a total grant income for 1988/89 of less than £50,000 and is based in, and carries out the majority of its activities in, England. Voluntary and professionally staffed organisations, but not local authorities or other statutory bodies, may apply. Special consideration will be given to projects in places where English Estates is active. (English Estates is an agency which builds and manages industrial and commercial property on behalf of the Department of Trade and Industry and the Rural Development Commission. It is engaged in projects in urban and rural areas.)

A very wide range of activities is eligible for the awards and 'the arts' will be interpreted in the broadest sense. Eligible programmes might include: residencies and placements, disability arts, celebrations, festivals and campaigns, reminiscence projects, black arts events and projects linked to education. Research, consultancies and feasibility studies are not eligible. The awards will range from £350 to £3500 and applicants may apply for any sum in this range. Projects will be assessed on their merits but judges will want to know the following:

- Does the project create new opportunities for arts work or extend existing ones?

- Does it show development in the applicant's own approach to the work?

- Are there new aspects to arts work in the project from which other organisations might learn?

- Is there a clearly identified relationship with the locality of the proposed project?

- Is the programme targetted to meet the needs of any particular sector within the community?

Judging is by a panel of people active in local arts projects and arts development and includes representatives of the organisers and sponsors.

For the first (1990) scheme projects must begin after 1st March 1990 and be completed by 31st August 1990. There are two deadlines for applications: 31st December 1989 for projects beginning after 1st March 1990 (first round) and 3rd March 1990 for projects beginning after 1st May 1990 (second round). Decisions will be announced on 7th February (first round) and 4th April (second round). One application may be submitted in each round but no organisation will receive more than one award.

Future: We assume that the future of this scheme will, in part, depend on the success of the first year.

Entry: Entry is on the basis of a fairly detailed application form which unusually but encouragingly includes an equal opportunities monitoring form designed to help the organisers assess the targeting of publicity for the scheme. The organisers specifically state that supporting material should not be sent with the initial application form. Short-listed projects will be asked to supply further information.

ASSOCIATION FOR INDUSTRIAL ARCHAEOLOGY AWARDS

The registered office of AIA is:
The Wharfage, Ironbridge, Telford, Shropshire TF8 7AW

According to their information leaflet The Association for Industrial Archaeology runs four competitions: The Dorothea Award for Conservation, the AIA Recording Award, the President's Award, and a Photographic Competition. Relatively limited information on these schemes is available. We assume that all AIA awards are open only to individual and institutional members of the Association and affiliated societies. Specific activities, including award schemes, may have different contact points to that given above.

FIELDWORK AND RECORDING AWARD

c/o Royal Commission on Ancient and Historic Monuments of Wales, Edleston House, Queen Street, Aberystwyth, Dyfed
Contact: Stephen Hughes

Each year the AIA offers an award (currently £100) to encourage high standards of fieldwork, surveys and archaeological recording. The Award is open to professional and amateur groups. Field reports and other relevant material should be submitted to the above address by the end of April. Presentations are made in September.

DOROTHEA AWARD FOR CONSERVATION

c/o 112 Milton Road, Fallings Park, Wolverhampton WV10 0ND

Contact: John Crompton, Executive Vice-President
Sponsor: Dorothea Restoration Engineers Ltd

This annual award, launched in 1984, offers a plaque and cheque (currently for £500), with commendations for runners-up, for appropriate and well-recorded conservation of the industrial, agricultural and domestic heritage which has been carried out by volunteers. This Award is open only to amateur (voluntary) groups and individuals. Closing date for entries is the end of May. The organisers have prepared some notes on Assessment and Recording in Conservation outlining the elements which the judges consider to be important to good practice in conservation. Past winners have included the Ruddington Framework Knitters Workshop, Jack and Jill Windmills Preservation Trust, and Staffordshire Industrial Archaeology Society.

Entry: On the official entry form together with supporting material.

PRESIDENT'S AWARD

We suggest you contact the AIA registered office for more information on the President's Award which is 'given annually to a site visited by delegates during the annual conference which is judged to have a high standard of interpretation and display'.

PHOTOGRAPHIC COMPETITION

We suggest you contact the AIA registered office for more information on this Competition which is designed to promote 'the photographic recording of historic industrial buildings, machinery and monuments.'

ASSOCIATION FOR THE PROTECTION OF RURAL SCOTLAND (APRS) AWARDS

The Association for the Protection of Rural Scotland, 14a Napier Road, Edinburgh EH10 5AY

Telephone: 031 229 1081

Contact: Robert L Smith, Director

APRS runs three main award schemes. These are the annual APRS Awards for buildings, structures and other physical works, which is the subject of this entry; Eyebright, an award for the rehabilitation of rural areas; and Eyebright Junior, a competition to encourage school children to improve local eyesores. The Eyebright competitions are covered in separate entries in this book.

The annual APRS award alternates its focus each year. In even years it is for new work and in odd years it is for reconstruction work. In both cases the eligibility criteria, entry and judging procedure and timetable are broadly similar. The overall function of the APRS Award is 'to encourage good planning and recognise particularly fine examples of structures (or works) built in a rural setting'. Each work is to be seen as making a definite contribution to the rural scene of Scotland. Works may include a single building, a group of buildings, a civil engineering structure or group of structures. The (odd year) reconstruction award also embraces landscaping of derelict areas and reclamation. Only schemes not in towns (defined as settlements with a population of 1500 or more) are eligible.

In both years, to be eligible, work must have been completed in the four years prior to 30th April of the year of entry. No work may be entered more than once, although a substantial second phase of a project previously submitted may be considered. Submissions may be made by any person, firm, organisation or central or local government authority.

There is one major award, a plaque for external or internal display, and certificates of merit and commendation are awarded at the discretion of the judges. The 1989 winner was the reconstruction of derelict farm buildings into a house at Muir of Blebo in Fife and the

1988 winner was the Kylesku Bridge. The deadline for entries is the end of June each year.

Future: The organisers state that 'the scheme will continue'.

Entry: On the official entry form with the following:

a) up to six full plate photographs;

b) a description of no more than 400 words;

c) an Ordnance Survey reference, clear site plan and sufficient floor plans, sections and elevations.

Photographs illustrating the site before the works were started would also be helpful.

THE AUGUSTINE COURTAULD AWARD

Rural Community Council of Essex, 79 Springfield Road, Chelmsford, Essex CM2 6JG

Telephone: 0245 352046

Contact: Director

This competition is administered by the Rural Community Council on behalf of the Trustees of the Augustine Courtauld Trust. It is designed to recognise groups that have 'done the most in their community to enhance, conserve or protect the natural environment of their area'. The organisers state that 'judges will place emphasis on imaginative schemes whose aims are to encourage an awareness of the environment, particularly amongst young people'.

The competition is open to 'any recognised group which is properly constituted in the county of Essex'. Both urban and rural groups and schools are eligible. Entrants must be able to show they they have planned their scheme and have made efforts to raise their own funds to carry the scheme to a conclusion.

The prizes are as follows: a first prize of £250 and a commemorative plaque to the best urban and rural schemes; a second prize of £100 to the runner-up in each category; and six prizes of £50 to groups, irrespective of their location, which merit commendation.

Prize money must be used in furtherance of the group's programme.

The closing date for the 1989/90 competition is 31st March 1990 and projects must have been started within the previous year. Judging of entries is scheduled for April and awards are to be presented at the Rural Comunity Council's AGM in July.

Future: We assume the competition will continue.

Entry: A written report, with photographs if possible, to be submitted with a completed entry form.

BARCLAYS YOUTH ACTION

Barclays Bank plc, Barclays Community Enterprise, PO Box 256, Fleetway House, 25 Farringdon Street, London, EC4A 4LP
Telephone: 071 489 1995

Contact: Brian Carr, Head of Barclays Community Enterprise
Sponsor: Barclays Bank plc

Although Barclays Youth Action is a grant scheme rather than a competition we thought that it was appropriate to include information in this book. The scheme is designed to 'asssist voluntary organisations who are promoting community service and enterprise by young people under 24 who have innovative and exciting ideas that are also practical. The scheme provides grants for projects in specific locations.' The following examples of types of projects which might be supported are given in the 'Guidelines for Applicants':

• Providing valuable community service for the elderly, disabled or others who are vulnerable or disadvantaged.

• Stimulating a sense of enterprise in the creation of purposeful employment opportunities for young people.

• Nurturing leadership and organisational skills relevant to work and community life in the 1980/90s.

• Renewing the environment of run-down areas.

High priority is given to new and imaginative ideas which are cost-effective, stimulate community development and directly involve young people in specific inner city or other areas with poor opportunities. Brian Carr stresses that wherever possible projects should '..involve young people themselves at all stages, from planning through to implementation, rather than simply provide services or facilities for the young.'

The printed information on the scheme states that to be eligible you should be a voluntary organisation with charitable status. However a covering letter suggests that groups without charitable status may be able to submit their application through an existing charity. Grants can cover such items as supervisory staff costs, volunteers expenses, other operating costs, training, equipment, vehicles, and materials for twelve months only. There is a limit of £15,000 on any single grant, although a project in several locations or a series of linked projects which are particularly imaginative and cost-effective may be able to exceed this figure.

There are three closing dates for applications during the year: 1st March, 1st June and 1st September. Applicants should be advised of the bank's decision within eight weeks of the relevant closing date. The activity for which the grant is required should be achievable within twelve months of receipt of the grant.

Future: This is a relatively new scheme and we have no reason to suggest that it will not remain an important part of Barclays' community enterprise programme for some time.

Entry: Applications must be on the official Application Form which among other things requires a fairly detailed breakdown of anticipated expenditure. Submission of additional material is not permitted – it will be requested if required.

BBC CHOIR GIRL OF THE YEAR

Network Producer, Religous Programmes, c/o BBC Radio York, Bootham Row, York YO3 7B

Telephone: 0904 641351

Contact: Julia Wills
Sponsor: BBC Radio

Julia Wills informs us that she is likely to remain the contact point for the 1990 competion but with the following address:

Religious Department, BBC, Broadcasting House, London W1A 1AA.

The Choir Girl of the Year competition aims to acknowledge and encourage the involvement of girls in British church choirs. Entry is open to girls aged between 12 and 17 (for the 1989 award aged over 12 on 16th April and under 17 on 9th September 1989) who are members of a bona-fide church choir singing regularly at services of worship.

Entrants submit a cassette tape of their singing to the National Organiser. The tape should contain one hymn and one other piece (anthem, oratorio-aria, or sacred song) of the entrant's choice. An expert panel then selects eight finalists. These are interviewed and appear on Good Morning Sunday and are again assessed by a panel of three judges. The overall winner receives a trophy, a personal prize of £250 and a Choristers Award for her choir.

Full or part-time students studying singing at a recognised institution are not eligible. Entrants must be authenticated by their minister, chaplain or choirmaster. Every entrant must be a practising member of a choir which sings weekly at a Sunday service.

In 1989 the closing date for entries was 21st July and the final took place on September 9th.

Future: The competition is certain to continue in 1990 although full details were not available at the time of writing.

Entry: On the official entry form with an audio cassette as outlined above.

BBC DESIGN AWARDS

The Design Council, 28 Haymarket, London, SW1Y 4SU
Telephone: 071 839 8000

Contact: Joanne Gwatkin-Williams, Awards Officer
Sponsor: Not yet confirmed

The BBC Design Awards, which were last run in 1987, are due to be re-launched in early January 1990. The organisation and rules and regulations of the competition are broadly similar to those which applied previously, with one major exception. This is that entry is now open to companies and other organisations situated anywhere in the world as long as the entry has been designed by a British designer working in the United Kingdom or abroad, or by a designer resident in the United Kingdom.

Entries must be submitted by the manufacturer, designer or producer of the design or by marketing organisations on their behalf. In the environment category entries are also acceptable from local authorities and other organisations responsible for the introduction of the submitted scheme. On the basis of the information available it would appear that the competition is open to charities and other voluntary organisations. We see no reason why books, catalogues, magazines, advertising, promotional leaflets, exhibitions and displays and other material produced for or by charities should not be eligible in the graphics category. Equally projects from environmental organisations and buildings for voluntary groups should be eligible for the environment category. The publicity generated by the scheme could be extremely valuable to organisations associated with the winning projects.

The three categories of entry are:

• Products: any product currently in production that can be purchased in the United Kingdom and used or worn by the general public;

• Environment: any designed environment in the United Kingdom to which the public has access is eligible. This includes office and workplace environments, townscapes, landscapes, buildings, community spaces, etc.

• Graphics: any two or three dimensional or moving graphics aimed at the British market. Corporate identity schemes, letter heads, packaging, logos, books, magazines, newspapers and posters are eligible.

The 1990 competition was launched in January 1990. The closing date for entries was the end of February, stage 1 judging (based on slides) took place in March and stage 2 judging (of hardware) in April/May. Programmes illustrating the judging process and showing the finalists are scheduled for June/July.

Public exhibitions of the finalists, at six regional venues, will take place during June/July. Final awards are made on the basis of voting by the public – as viewers of the television programmes or visitors to the exhibitions. In 1987 the public voters were encouraged to judge the finalists on the basis of function (does it do its job well?), appearance (is it attractive?), materials (have they been used effectively?), and cost (is the price of the final product right?).

Future: Continuation of the competition beyond 1990 is unlikely to be confirmed for some time.

Entry: Full details are available from the Design Council.

BEST KEPT VILLAGE COMPETITIONS

Best Kept Village Competitions are organised in virtually every shire county in England and Wales – in the majority of cases by the county rural comunity council or county branch of the Council for the Protection of Rural England. The county organisers of the competitions are listed below. Further information on the competitions is also available from ACRE and CPRE:

ACRE (Action with Communities in Rural England) Stroud Road, Cirencester, Glos GL7 6JR
Telephone: 0285 653477

CPRE (Council for the Protection of Rural England) White House, 25 Buckingham Palace Road, London SW1W 0PP
Telephone: 071 235 9481

Sponsors: The majority of county competitions are sponsored by Calor Gas Ltd, but there are several competitions which have other commercial sponsors.

Best Kept Village Competitions are a well established 'institution' in rural England and Wales – the first, in Gloucestershire, was set up in the 1920s. They are designed to foster community spirit and local pride and encourage action to improve the environment. Organisers take great pains to stress the fundamental ethos of their competitions which award '...not the most beautiful, not the most ancient, not the most picturesque, just the best kept..'.

Most competitions have at least two categories of entry based on village (or parish) population size. Some break down entries even further. Essex, for example, has four classes, for parishes with under 300, 300-800, 800 to 2000, and over 2000 population. But the exact categories and definitions vary considerably from county to county. In addition most BKV competitions will embrace more specific 'targetted' awards – the Calor Conservation Award, for particular conservation projects, and the Calor Most Improved Village Award for example. Some incorporate awards for the 'Best Kept Village Hall', 'Best Burial Ground', 'Best Village Noticeboard' and even 'Best Telephone Kiosk' in the overall competition. (Some counties have a Best Village Hall competition – see separate entry.)

The awards themselves vary from county to county. The most common practice is for winners to receive a sign or plaque which is held for a year and either a modest prize of cash or goods. Benches, bulbs and trees are common prizes. In Clwyd, the £150 cash prize to winners must go towards the completion of an 'approved improvement project'. However, for most entrants, the physical value of the award will be immaterial – the competition's value lies in the status afforded to winners. Many competitions are fiercely contested.

Most competitions do not specify who may or may not enter. In most cases it will be a recognised local organisation such as the parish council, Women's Institute, amenity society or village hall committee which submits the formal entry, although most would hope to engage the active support of other groups, businesses and individuals.

The timing of the competitions varies from county to county. Most organisers publicise their competition in the early Spring, inviting entries by late Spring or early summer. Judging normally takes place during the summer months with awards announced and presented during September or October.

Future: While the details may change from year to year, we anticipate that all competitions will continue in their existing form for at least the next few years.

Entry: Contact the appropriate county organiser for details. Most will have an official entry form and in most, but not all, cases there is no entry fee.

County Organisers:

Avon: Mrs Dorrie Ellis, Avon CPRE, Hillside, The Common, Felton, Bristol, BS18 7YN Tel: 027587 2549

Bedfordshire: Bedfordshire Rural Community Council, The Old School, Cardington, Bedford, MK44 3SX Tel: 0234 838771/2

Berkshire: Mr F Jupp, BKV Organiser, Springfields, 59 Stockcross, Newbury, RG16 8LJ Tel: 048 838 625

Buckinghamshire: Richard Pushman, BKV Coordinator, Umtata, Naphill Common, High Wycombe, Bucks, HO14 4SZ Tel: 024024 4152

Cambridgeshire: Cambridgeshire Community Council, Cambridgeshire House, 7 Hills Road, Cambridge CB2 1NL Tel: 0223 350666

Cheshire: Cheshire Community Council, 96 Lower Bridge Street, Chester, CH1 1RU Tel: 0244 322188/323602

Cornwall: T Selwood, Secretary, Cornwall Branch CPRE, 62, Boxwell Park, Bodmin, Cornwall

Cumbria: Voluntary Action Cumbria, Birbeck House, Duke Street, Penrith, Cumbria, CA11 7NA Tel: 0768 68086

Derbyshire: Frank Constable, BKV Organiser, Derbyshire RCC, Church Street, Wirksworth, Derby, DE4 4EY Tel: 062982 4797

Devon: Mrs P Parker, Hon Secretary Devon CPRE, Knowles House, Kentisbeare, Cullompton, Devon EX15 2E11 Tel: 088 46 325

Dorset: Dorset Community Council, 57 High West Street, Dorchester, DT1 1UT Tel: 0305 62270

Durham: Mrs Pauline Purvis, Organiser, Durham County Tidy Village Competition, 10 Whitwell Acres, High Stincliffe, County Durham, DH1 2PX

Essex: Rural Community Council for Essex, 79 Springfield Road, Chelmsford, Essex CM2 6JG Tel: 0245 352046

Gloucestershire: Gloucestershire Branch CPRE, Community House, College Green, Gloucester GL1 2LZ Tel: 0452 28491

Hampshire: Hampshire Council of Community Service, Beaconsfield House, Andover Road, Winchester, SO22 6AT Tel: 0962 54971

Hereford and Worcester:
  Worcestershire: Brigadier Young, Worcestershire CPRE, The Old House, Clifton on Teme, Worcester, Tel: 088 65 301
  Herefordshire: Ben Nash, Herefordshire CPRE, Old Orchard, Little Dewchurch, Hereford HR2 6PS Tel: 043270 287

Hertfordshire: Brigadier F M De Butts, Hon. Director, The Hertfordshire Society, 29a Mill Lane, Welwyn, Herts AL6 9EU, Tel: 043871 7587

Humberside: Community Council of Humberside, 14 Market Place, Howden, Goole, N. Humberside DN14 7BJ Tel: 0430 430904

Isle of Wight: Mrs A M Finlay, Hon. Secretary, BKV Committee, Culebra, St Helens, Isle of Wight, PO33 1TN

Kent: Kent Rural Community Council, 15 Manor Road, Folkestone, Kent, CT20 2AH Tel: 0303 52333

Lancashire: Community Council of Lancashire, 15 Victoria Road, Fulwood, Preston, Lancashire, PR2 4PS Tel: 0772 717461

Leicestershire: Leicestershire Rural Community Council, 133 Loughborough Road, Leicester, LE4 5LX Tel: 0533 662905

Lincolnshire: Lincolnshire CPRE, c/o Community Council of Lincolnshire, 1 Kesteven Street, Sleaford, Lincolnshire, NG34 7DT Tel: 0529 302466

Norfolk: Organiser, Best Kept Village Competition, Planning and Property Department, Norfolk County Council, County Hall, Martineau Lane, Norwich NR1 2DH Tel: 0603 611122

Northamptonshire: Northamptonshire Rural Community Council, Hunsbury Hill Centre, Harksome Hill, Northampton, NN4 9QX Tel: 0604 765888

Northumberland: Community Council of Northumberland, Tower Buildings, 9 Oldgate, Morpeth, NE61 1PT Tel: 0670 517178

Nottinghamshire: Nottinghamshire Branch CPRE, c/o Notts Rural Community Council, Minster Chambers, Church Street, Southwell, NG25 0HD Tel: 0636 815267

Oxfordshire: Oxfordshire Rural Community Council, The Hadow Rooms, 101 Banbury Road, Oxford, OX2 6NE Tel: 0865 512488

Shropshire: Community Council for Shropshire, 1 College Hill, Shrewsbury, SY1 1LT Tel: 0743 60641

Somerset: Community Council for Somerset, St Margaret's, Hamilton Road, Taunton, TA1 2EG Tel: 0823 331222/3

Staffordshire: Community Council of Staffordshire, St Georges, Corporation Street, Stafford, ST16 3AG Tel: 0785 42525

Suffolk: Community Council for Suffolk, Alexandra House, Rope Walk, Ipswich, IP4 1LZ Tel: 0473 230000

Surrey: Surrey Voluntary Service Council, Jenner House, 2 Jenner Road, Guildford, GU1 3PN Tel 0483 66072

East and West Sussex: Sussex Rural Community Council, Sussex House, 212 High Street, Lewes, BN7 2NH Tel: 0273 473422

Warwickshire: Warwickshire Rural Community Council, The Abbotsford, 10 Market Place, Warwick, CV34 4SL Tel: 0926 499596

Wiltshire: Mr C J Bradish, Wiltshire CPRE, Sutherlands, The Green, Pitton, Salisbury, SP5 1DZ Tel: 0380 2157

Yorkshire: Yorkshire Rural Community Council, William House, Skipton Road, Skelton, York, YO3 6WZ Tel: 0904 645271 (The Yorkshire competition does not cover the whole county each year – in any particular year only certain districts will be included).

Clwyd: Clwyd Voluntary Services Council, Fford yr Orsaf, Ruthin, Clwyd, LL15 1BP Tel: 08242 2441/3805

Dyfed: Dyfed Association of Voluntary Services, 11/12 King Street, Carmarthen, Dyfed, SA31 1BH Tel: 0267 236367

South Glamorgan: A J Charles, Hon Secretary, BKV in Vale of Glamorgan, 43 Broadway, Cowbridge, South Glamorgan, CP7 7EK

BEST OF BRITISH YOUTH AWARDS

Further information:
National Council of YMCAs, 640 Forest Road, London E17 3DZ
Telephone: 081 520 5599

Nominations to:
YMCA/Today Best of British Youth Awards, Today Programme, BBC Broadcasting House, London W1A 4WW

Sponsor: National Westminster Bank

This scheme aims to 'identify young people between the ages of 16 and 21 who are making the most of their own lives and the lives of those around them'. Nominations can be made by and for any UK citizen (except those with connections with the Today programme). The publicity leaflet for the awards illustrates the breadth of potential nominations in the following words – 'Many young people all over Britain are making a real impact. Some are involved in community work, or have started special projects or campaigns. Others have shown great determination in overcoming a disadvantage or have excelled in the arts or sport, helping others at the same time.' All are eligible.

Nominations are made by members of the public including listeners to the Today programme. From these nominations six finalists are chosen by a celebrity panel and are featured on Today. Listeners to the programme then vote for the winners. The prizes in 1989 were:

First: £1000 for the winner's chosen youth project or charity and £400 personal prize;
Second: £500 for the chosen project/charity and £300 personal prize;
Third: £250 for the chosen project/charity and £200 personal prize.
Prizes were also awarded to other finalists and short-listed candidates.

The scheme is launched in early spring and the six finalists are featured on Radio Four's Today programme in June. The prizes are presented at a 'celebrity lunch' at London's Savoy Hotel in August.

Future: We assume this scheme will continue.

Entry: Nominations, including a description up to 500 words on the nominee, should be sent to the Today programme at the above address. Leaflets and posters are available from the National Council of YMCAs.

BEST SOCIAL INVENTIONS PRIZE

The Institute for Social Inventions, 24 Abercorn Place, London NW8 9XP
Telephone: 071 229 7253

Contact: none given

Each year the Institute for Social Inventions offers awards, publicity and £1000 in prize money for the best social inventions proposed by members of the public. A social invention is defined as a new and imaginative solution to a social problem, or a new way of improving the quality of life – for instance a new social service, a new way for people to relate to each other, a new organisational structure, or a new combination of existing ideas. New products, technological inventions or patentable devices are excluded.

Previous winners of the competition have included proposals for: wildlife areas around hospitals; splitting comprehensive schools into mini-schools; fruit growing 'forest gardens'; a new university run by the unemployed; a solar village in Wales; 'cake-sharing' disarmament; and a Swiss-style cantonisation scheme for South Africa.

The prize money is divided amongst the following categories at the judges' discretion:

i) Ideas;

ii) Projects underway;

iii) Projects underway abroad that could be (or are being) tried in the UK;

iv) Ideas and projects suggested by young people under 18 years. (which may be accompanied by A4 drawings).

The following is a summary of the main criteria considered by the judges although entrants are not required to meet them all:

• Is the project new (to the UK) and imaginative?

• Will it improve the quality of life or create a more human scale society?

• Are there signs of progress? Have efforts been made to implement it? What response has there been?

- Does it have a sound structure with a potential for being self-supporting or for self-growth?
- Is it designed to be grass roots?
- Will it have lasting results?
- Will it benefit a large number of people?
- What are its chances of success?

The deadline each year is 1st June and winners are announced in the media by the end of June.

Future: The competition is an important part of the Institute's work and seems well established.

Entry: There is no entry fee or form. Entries should be a maximum of 1000 words although supporting material may be sent. Entries should be accompanied by a signed and witnessed statement, testifying that the idea has not been copied from elsewhere (except category (iii) above). Entries in categories (i) and (iii) should be supported by evidence that entrants have sought expert opinion and the reactions of those affected by the idea or who would have to carry it out. Any objections would need to be answered by entrants.

BET CHORISTERS AWARDS

BET Chorister Awards Office, BET PLC, Stratton House, Piccadilly London W1X 6AS

Telephone: 071 629 8886

Contact: Christopher Legge, corporate communication manager
Sponsors: BET PLC and Royal School of Church Music

BET Choristers Awards were founded to further the cause and quality of young choristers' singing. They are designed to foster and encourage young parish church choristers and help lift standards.

There are two main awards: The BET Choirboy of the Year and The BET Choirgirl of the Year. The former is for boys aged 9 – 13 and has been running for over fifteen years, the latter, for girls aged 10 – 14 was established more recently. (The BBC Choirgirl of the Year Competition for older girls, aged 13 – 17 has a separate entry in this book.)

The awards are relatively substantial and could be extremely valuable to the choirs with which the individual choristers are associated. The first prize is £250 for the winning chorister plus £2000 for his/her choir. The second and third prizes are £100/£500 and £50/£250 respectively. All finalists receive a small cash prize and all contestants receive a personal certificate of achievement. The organisers anticipate that the winner and possibly other contestants will receive considerable publicity and opportunities for public performance and recordings. Indeed the organisers arrange for winners to receive the services of a professional agency for a period following the announcement of the awards.

Entrants are initially required to submit a tape recording of their singing. On the basis of these, semi-finalists are selected by the Royal School of Church Music for judging of live performance at eight regional locations and then subsequently at a final which is followed immediately by the Awards Dinner and Presentation.

Both the boys and girls awards are run in parallel and to the same timetable. Entries are accepted between January and April. Regional finals are held between May and July, and the National Final and Awards Presentation is held in October.

It is noteworthy that BET's support for these awards is a reflection of a much broader commitment to raising standards of choir singing in the United Kingdom. For example the company helps provide places for young church choristers on Royal School of Church Music residential courses and has commissioned new Choristers Carols. Interestingly the company has also commissioned research to discover how their awards can best help the cause of young choristers' singing.

Future: BET's commitment to supporting young choristers appears extremely strong and the company seems determined to maintain its involvement.

Entry: By official entry form enclosing a tape recording and if possible a black and white photograph.

BRECKNOCK COMMUNITY ENVIRONMENTAL PROJECT COMPETITION

Brecknock Borough Council, Cambrian Way, The Watton, Brecon, LD3 7HR

Telephone: 0874 4141 ext 283

Contact: Catherine James

This competition, actively supported by the Brecknock Wildlife Trust, was first established in 1988 and is organised annually. It aims to encourage community projects which lead to visual improvement in a locality or help conserve or encourage wildlife habitats. Entrants must be able to demonstrate 'an end benefit to the local community'.

The scheme is a combination of a competitive grant scheme and a conventional competition in that it appears to provide awards and prizes for project proposals as well as completed schemes. There are five awards of £100 each, one for each local authority division (Brecon, Builth Wells, Ystradgynlais, Hay-on-Wye and Crickhowell). The Kyle Cup is also awarded to the best school entry. The competition is open to community councils (equivalent of English parish councils), primary schools and other recognised community groups. A project may be on public or private land but must be located where the general public can benefit from or have access to it. Tree planting, footpath works, rubbish clearance, stone wall repairs, village trails and painting community buildings are just some of the types of project regarded as eligible.

The 1989/90 Competition required entries to be submitted by 24th November 1989 with prizewinners announced in December to allow work to commence in January 1990. However projects commenced or completed after 1st January 1989 were eligible.

Future: We assume the scheme will continue.

Entry: On a very straightforward entry form.

BRITAIN IN BLOOM

c/o The Tidy Britain Group, The Pier, Wigan, WN3 4EX
Telephone: 0942 824620

Contact: Coordinator, Britain in Bloom
(Initial contact should be with regional organisers – see below)
Sponsors: National sponsors are being sought. Various local sponsors.

'Britain in Bloom is a nationwide campaign to make our cities, towns and villages even more beautiful by using plants, trees, shrubs and flowers and imaginative landscaping..'. The competition is designed to encourage 'the conservation of pleasant natural features, the embellishment of man-made areas and the screening or removal of eyesores in industrial quarters.' The competition is heavily promoted by regional tourist boards and other organisations with a strong interest in tourism. It is organised along similar lines each year.

The competition is for places – cities, towns and villages – and entries are submitted by district, borough, town or parish (or in Wales community) councils or by 'the approved local organising committee'. However most entrants will want to secure the active support and involvement of local organisations, businesses, public authorities and individuals.

The competition has two main stages. In England, entries are submitted to the appropriate regional organisation (generally a regional tourist board) which undertakes the initial judging and then submits winning entries to the Britain in Bloom competition organised by The Tidy Britain Group. In Scotland, Wales, Northern Ireland, Isle of Man and Jersey, the 'regional' winners are entered directly into Britain in Bloom. However the competition does not stop there, for 'each year two eligible winning finalists in Britain in Bloom are put forward to compete with their European counterparts and stand a chance of international honours'.

There are eight entry categories: large city, city, large town, town, small town, urban village/community, large village and village. Population size defines the categories except for urban villages/communities. Britain in Bloom winners receive a trophy. In addition there are numerous national and regional awards for particular types of entry.

Judges look for: overall floral impact, general enthusiasm and commitment, actual achievement in the light of local circumstances, public sector, individual and corporate effort, improvements since the previous year, absence of litter and photographic evidence of Spring planting. The organisers stress that 'winners will be those who are supported by all sections of the community.'

Future: Britain in Bloom is very well established and looks most unlikely to be discontinued in the foreseeable future.

Entry: Entries must be submitted on the official application form provided by the appropriate regional or national organiser – listed below:

England

East Midlands	0604 27878
East Anglia	0603 762888
South East England	0273 677321
Southern England	0703 620006
West Country	0392 874979
Heart of England	0905 613132
Yorkshire & Humberside	0532 734184
North West England	0204 591511
Cumbria	0768 68086
Northumbria	0661 23226
Thames and Chilterns	0993 779208
London	0483 797223
Isle of Man (Tourist Board)	0624 74323
Jersey (Jersey Tourism)	0534 31210
Northern Ireland (Tourist Board)	0232 231221
Scotland (Beautiful Scotland in Bloom)	078682 4536/5428
Wales (Wales in Bloom Foundation)	0492 531859

THE BUSINESS AND INDUSTRY ENVIRONMENT AWARDS

Business and Industry Commitment to the Environment, c/o Business in the Community, 227a City Road, London EC1V 1LX
Telephone: 071 253 3716

Contact: Tony Shillingford, Secretary, Environment Awards

The scheme, which has been run since 1975, aims to reward 'initiative and innovation across virtually the whole spectrum of industrial development and activity and the management of natural resources', and give 'public recognition to projects which display genuine commitment to the preservation and improvement of the environment backed by evidence of a strong sense of social responsibility.'

The brochure for the scheme cites holiday villages, urban renewal schemes, power stations, canals, public houses and small workshops as just some of the types of eligible project. It states that 'literally any environmentally inspired undertaking can compete on equal terms with new factory, office, warehousing and retail developments whether new or restored.' Projects may 'concern an actual workspace ...or... involve the preservation or enhancement of the community and general infrastructure within which industry or commerce operates'. They should indicate the company's commitment to and policy of environmental responsibility.

The awards are open to both the public and private sector. Entries are invited from both large and small companies. While the majority of awards go to private companies, past winners have included statutory agencies (for example British Rail, Water authorities), local authorities (Swansea City Council won a Premier Award in 1988 for their Maritime Quarter project) and voluntary organisations (Southwark Environment Trust were commended in 1988). The Assessors make five Premier Awards and ten Major Commendations each year.

The deadline for entries in 1989 was 30th June. All entries are then personally visited by the Assessors, all experienced people from business or specialist agencies (such as Nature Conservancy Council), and in 1989 all men. Award winners are notified in the autumn and invited to an Award Ceremony in London at the end of the year.

Future: The Awards will continue in 1990.

Entry: Unusually there is no official entry form. The organisers say that a 'succinct written presentation supported by any relevant drawings, photographs or videos will suffice.' Architects and other professional advisors may only submit entries on behalf of their clients with their prior agreement.

CARING IN THE COMMUNITY

Scottish Post Office Board, West Port House, 102 West Port, Edinburgh, EH3 9HS

Telephone: 031 228 7278

Contact: Chairman's Office
Sponsor: Scottish Post Office Board

This scheme succeeds the Andrew Carnegie Scheme which the Scottish Post Office Board sponsored between 1986 and 1988. The new award scheme provides financial support of up to £5000 for an imaginative proposal for voluntary work in each of these five broad categories of care: children, elderly, disability, environment and an open category (covering voluntary work not readily identifiable with the other categories). The main purpose of each award is to make funds available for a future activity or project which would not otherwise be undertaken.

The awards are for voluntary organisations operating in Scotland. Those which have already attracted charitable, or local government funding or which represent national bodies locally are eligible to apply. Applicants need to show: that they have charitable status, the sources and extent of existing finance, that if the cost of the project is more than the amount of the award that complementary finance is assured, and that if successful they are prepared to participate in a public presentation. Judges in 1989/90 included individuals associated with the Scottish Post Office Board, the Carnegie UK Trust, Grampian Regional Council and the Scottish Council for Voluntary Organsiations.

Entries were to be submitted by 12th January 1990 and awards were due to be made before 31st March 1990.

Future: A new scheme which we assume will be continued if the first year is successful.

Entry: Submission of proposals (maximum of four sides of A4 double-space typed) with appropriate supporting material. There is no application form although Guidelines for Applicants are available.

CHARITY ANNUAL REPORT AND ACCOUNTS AWARD

Accountancy (Journal of the Institute of Chartered Accountants in England and Wales), 40 Bernard Street, London WC1N 1LD

Telephone: 071 628 7060

Contact: Geoffrey Holmes, Editor (Managing)
Sponsors: Accountancy (Journal), Charities Aid Foundation and the Charity Forum.

The Awards, which have been run annually since 1983, are designed to 'encourage charities to publish better annual reports and accounts, which do not merely fulfill the requirement for a record of stewardship but which make a positive communication to members, donors and potential donors on behalf of the charity'. The competition is open to all donation-seeking charities within the British Isles (so we assume Eire is included). However, Citizens Advice Bureaux and similar organisations are not eligible.

In 1989 there were three prizes – £1500 for the overall winner and £750 each for the best report and accounts from a charity with an income under £1,000,000 and for the charity with an income of under £100,000. Commendations may also be awarded to entrants considered to be of special merit. Awards are presented at a special ceremony in December. Winners commonly attract publicity in the national media – in itself an incentive to enter the competition. In 1988 there were 500 entries. The winners were Guide Dogs for the Blind Association, Mary Rose Trust, Council for the Protection of Rural England and Greater Bristol Trust.

Judges look for: general readability, design and clarity of presentation, compliance with accepted accounting practice and the overall 'honesty' of the way the accounts are presented within the document. The size and possibly limited resources of the charity are taken into account, particularly for the two restricted categories.

Note that entries must comprise both the annual report and audited accounts. Where there is a single document containing only abbreviated accounts, it must be supported by unabridged audited accounts. Report and accounts will be considered as one unit: one without the other will render the entry ineligible.

The deadline for the 1989 competition was 31st August 1989.

Future: We expect the competition to continue in future years.

Entry: On the official (but very brief) entry form together with two copies of the annual report and accounts.

CHILD OF ACHIEVEMENT AWARDS

McDonald's Child of Achievement Awards, PO Box 86, Weybridge, Surrey KT13 9JX
Telephone: 0932 850006

Contact: Julie Fisher
Sponsor: McDonalds

The Child of Achievement Awards are presented to 'children up to the age of 16 who by their everyday tasks help others, or who by their ability to overcome personal illness or disability ' are worthy of national recognition and honour. They have been run annually since 1983, and at present are sponsored and heavily promoted by McDonalds. Children can be nominated for the award by any individual including members of their family. One hundred and fifty children are honoured with a 'Child of Achievement Award' each year. Awards for this 'prestigous' award are presented at a 'glittering ceremony' at London's 'glorious' Guildhall.

As well as awarding children who regularly help others (a disabled brother or sister for example) or who have overcome adversity, the scheme also honours children who undertake group projects such as raising money for charity or environmental projects. The organisers say that there are 'no restrictions save that the project be achieved by children'.

Although the Awards themselves have no monetary or physical value, except in terms of the publicity generated for winners and the projects with which they are associated, the organisers of the Awards have also established the Child of Achievement Trust Fund. The Fund exists to 'enable children to achieve more'. It provides financial help to families and children in need and has supported a range of national and local organisations, appeals and projects. For the next two years (from 1989), 50% of the Fund's financial support will go to establishing the Ronald McDonald House for parents of sick children at Guy's Hospital. The trustees of the Fund actively seek contributions to it from individuals and corporate organisations.

The 1989/90 Awards required nominations to be submitted by 8th December 1989.

Future: We assume the Awards will continue for the foreseeable future.

Entry: Nominations on the official entry form or by letter. Nominators are required to describe the reasons for their nomination in just 50 words.

CIVIC/ ARCHITECTURAL DESIGN AWARDS

There are numerous competitions and award schemes which recognise and promote high standards in building and architectural design. Most of these are organised by local authorities (normally district or borough councils), local amenity or civic societies. Some of these schemes embrace environmental and conservation projects undertaken by communities or voluntary groups. Those that do, and of which we are aware, are included in this book, but those schemes that are normally only concerned with the design of structures and buildings or their surroundings do not have separate entries. However those national and local schemes on which we have information are simply listed below.

National Awards

The Civic Trust Awards for excellence in architecture, planning, civic and landscape design.
Organised by: The Civic Trust, 17 Carlton House Terrace, London, SW1Y 5AW Telephone: 071 930 0914

The Commercial Property Landscape Awards
Organised by: Jackson-Stops & Staff, 14 Curzon Street, London W1Y 7FH Telephone: 071 499 6291
Contact: Giles Harbottle, Director of Public Relations

Local Awards

Aylesbury Good Design Award
Organised by: The Aylesbury Society, 8 Broughton Close, Bierton, Aylesbury, Bucks, HP22 5DJ
Contact: Roger King, Honorary Secretary

Bath Environmental Awards
Organised by: Bath Conservation Area Advisory Committee, Chief Executive's Department, Bath City Council, Guildhall, Bath BA1 5AW Telephone: 0225 461111 ext 2417
Contact: Mr D J Taylor, Senior Administrator

Chester Shop Front Design Award
Organised by: Chester Civic Trust, 18 Devonshire Place, Handbridge, Chester, CH4 7BZ Telephone: 0244 676814
Contact: Stephen Langtree

The Royal Borough of Kensington and Chelsea Environment Award
Organised by: Department of Planning and Transportation, The Royal Borough of Kensington and Chelsea, The Town Hall, Hornton Street, London W8 7NX Telephone: 071 937 5464
Contact: Director of Planning and Transportation

North Hertfordshire District Council Civic Award
Organised by: North Hertfordshire District Council, Couincil Offices, Gernon Road, Letchworth, Herts, SG6 3JF Telephone: 0462 686500
Contact: Director of Planning

North Warwickshire Borough Council Civic Award
Organised by: North Warwickshire Borough Council, PO Box 6, The Council House, South Street, Atherstone, Warwickshire, CV9 1BG

Tel: 0827 715341
Contact: Borough Planning Officer

South Tyneside Council Good Design Awards
Organised by: South Tyneside Metropolitan Borough Council, Planning Department, Town Hall, Westoe Road, South Shields, NE33 2RL Telephone: 091 42717

THE COLONEL SANDERS ENVIRONMENTAL AWARDS

c/o Reginald Watts Associates, 1-11 Hay Hill, London W1X 7LF
Telephone: 071 491 2121

Contact: Victoria Sabin
Sponsor: Kentucky Fried Chicken in association with the Tidy Britain Group

This scheme, which has been run since 1977, aims to encourage all sections of the community to take action to tidy up Britain. The range of projects which may be entered is very wide – the key criterion is that a project must demonstrate a positive contribution to improving the environment. Projects in the United Kingdom are eligible.

There are four categories of entry:

- local authorities (which we assume includes parish and town councils)
- voluntary groups
- schools and youth groups in the 11-18 age group
- schools and youth groups in the under 11 age group.

Projects are judged on originality, effort and initiative as well as achievement. Any project, large or small, which shows thought and imagination will be considered. Possible projects include: an anti-litter campaign, tree and flower planting, waste recycling and graffiti removal.

The entry and judging procedure is as follows. Potential entrants first register their intention to enter a project. A written report of the project (and other material) must then be submitted. The panel of judges reviews entries and selects a shortlist of five finalists in each category. These finalists are invited to Finals Day in London at which they are asked to make a brief presentation about their project and answer questions. The presentation of the awards then takes place at a reception at the House of Commons. The winner in each category receives a trophy and £500, second prize is £250, third prize £150 and the other finalists receive £75 each. All finalists receive a certificate of merit. Local authority finalists are expected to donate their prize to a suitable charity or towards sponsoring litterbins in their area.

In 1989 entries had to be submitted by 25th October with Finals Day scheduled for 28th November.

Future: We assume this scheme will continue.

Entry: Initial registration on the official form. The submission itself should comprise a written report and may also include supporting material such as photographs, cuttings, slides and audio or video tapes.

COMMUNITY CARE ENTERPRISE AWARDS

Community Care (magazine), Carew House, Wallington, Surrey, SM6 0DX

Telephone: 081 661 3500

Contact: Marketing Department

The organisers have asked us to include the following statement:

'These Awards are made each year to assist new and innovative projects in the statutory and voluntary social services. Awards are not made to support existing schemes but rather to assist new ones to come into being. Application can only be made upon completion of entry forms supplied by the magazine when full details are published in Community Care in the Spring.'

The following information is taken from the published details for the 1989 Awards. This scheme, which has been running since 1986, provides awards of up to £2500 for projects which make major contributions towards effective use of resources in social work. Entries may be submitted by anyone employed in the statutory or voluntary social services as well as teachers and students on CSS or CQSW courses. Entries will be accepted from individuals and groups and teams. Schemes can be large or small. Awards cannot be made to existing projects but they may be used as 'seed money' to get an idea off the ground and help attract funding from elsewhere.

The 1988 winners included: National Childrens Homes Wales for a schools training package concerning mental handicap, Denise Hill (a Cheshire Community Worker) for a project for sending students on training courses aimed at teaching people with learning difficulties how to communicate effectively, Royal National Institute for the Deaf for a training project, Radnor and District Mental Health Association for a mobile disco to be operated by people with mental and social disorders, Newry and Mourne Carers Support Group for an information pack, and Avon Social Service Department for video equipment to produce a video magazine for people with a mental handicap.

Judges in 1989 were Terry Philpott (Editor of Community Care), and three other experts from the statutory, voluntary and academic sectors. Entries had to be submitted by 4th September 1989. Winning projects must be operating within six months of receiving the award.

Winning schemes will be followed through by a Community Care staff writer.

Future: This scheme will operate in 1990 and, we assume, beyond.

Entry: Applications must be accompanied by a completed entry form. Forms are published in Community Care in the Spring. Submissions themselves should comprise a written proposal of a maximum of 1000 words, a detailed costing and a 'manager's statement' stating that the idea can be put into practice if it wins an award.

COMMUNITY PARTNERSHIP PRIZE

Community Projects Foundation, 60 Highbury Grove, London N5 2AG
Telephone: 071 226 5375

Contact: Dorrett Crooks
Sponsor: Barclays Bank

This prize was offered in 1989 to celebrate the Community Project Foundation's twenty first anniversary. An unusual feature of the scheme was that it was promoted both independently and as part of the Times/RIBA Community Enterprise Awards. (See separate entry). CPF (and Barclays) were responsible for assessing Partnership Prize winners although the prizes themselves were presented at The Times/RIBA Awards ceremony. In 1990 the Prize will an integral part of The Times/RIBA Community Enterprise Scheme.

The purpose of the Community Partnership Prize is '.. to recognise the achievements of community groups in bringing about worthwhile changes in their community...' The organisers state that '... any community group can enter. We are looking for examples of partnerships that have improved a local community, partnerships between black and white, or young and old....partnerships between a group and a local authority or a company. The winners will be groups that can demonstrate successful and imaginative partnerships that have brought benefits to the whole community.'

In 1989 a first prize of £1000 and second and third prizes of £500 each were awarded and about 150 entries were received. The winner of the first prize was Antur Waunfawr, a co-operative project in Gwynedd, north Wales. Set up in 1983, the project provides employment and housing for physically and mentally handicapped people in a way which fully involves them in village life. Second and third prizes went to Salt Meadows Play and Environment Project in Gateshead and West Walker Community Developments in Newcastle upon Tyne, the latter also the winner of a special award under The Times/RIBA scheme sponsored by the National Childrens Play and Recreation Unit.

The publicity material specifically for the 1989 Community Partnership Prize simply asked entrants to submit a two to three page letter describing 'your group, its membership and its activities...[and] how long you have been going, how many supporters you have, how many users there are of the facilities that you provide.' Entrants were also asked to say 'what you think is special about your partnership, how it started and, above all, the way it has helped to benefit the community..' and to submit an annual report and other supporting material. There was no need to complete an entry form for the Community Partnership Prize although this was required of entrants to The Times/RIBA scheme.

Future: The Prize will be awarded in 1990 as an integral part of The Times/RIBA Community Enterprise Scheme.

Entry: Check current arrangements with Community Projects Foundation address above.

COMMUNITY PLANNING AWARDS

The Royal Town Planning Institute, 26 Portland Place, London W1N 4BE
Telephone: 071 636 9107

Contact: Tony Garvey
National Council for Voluntary Organisations, 26 Bedford Square, London WC1B 3HU
Telephone: 071 636 4066

This scheme, which was first run in 1988, is organised jointly by NCVO and RTPI. We understand that the competition will be run in 1990, but as further details are not yet available, we have included information on the 1988 scheme as a guide to the future.

The 1988 Community Planning Awards were given to organisations and informal groups judged to be the most effective in influencing the following:

- the preparation of a local authority's development plan;
- the procedures for handling planning applications;
- a particular development proposal;
- the use of public land;
- the exercise of discretionary powers;
- other ways of changing statutory mechanisms or proposals for the better.

In 1988 the first prize was £1000 and the second and third prizes £250 each. The 1988 competition attracted over 120 entries. Twenty six entries were shortlisted by the three judges (two from RTPI, one from NCVO) and of these the West End Environmental Group gained first prize for securing the Rally Community Park in Leicester against the threat of development. Second prize went to Lye Business for the economic and social rejuvenation of the town of Lye in the West Midlands and third prize went to Furness Improvement and Development Organisation in Halifax.

Entries were required by 30th April 1988 and judging took place over the following months. Awards were finally made in April/May 1989.

Future: The competition will run in 1990, but full details are not yet available.

Entry: In 1988, on the official form plus unrestricted supporting material.

COMMUNITY PRIDE AWARDS

Civic Trust, 17 Carlton House Terrace, London SW1Y 5AW
Telephone: 071 930 0914

Contact: Arthur Percival/Sue Wright
Sponsor: British Telecom

The Community Pride Awards were launched in August 1989. British Telecom's sponsorship will ensure the scheme runs for at least three years. The Awards are exclusively for the 1000 or so local amenity societies registered with the Civic Trust all of whom should automatically receive details of the scheme. Unlike many 'awards', this scheme is for project proposals and ideas – the organisers specifically state that 'there is no point in entering a project you've already started. The Awards are not intended to recognise the worth of schemes already underway or completed..'

The only criteria are that 'entries should improve the local scene and must be completed within two years of winning an Award.' The organisers appear to be genuinely keen to encourage a very wide range of entries. They cite the restoration of a building, reclamation of wasteland, creation of a new amenity such as seating on a village green or a visitor centre and a landscaping scheme as just some examples of potential winners. The Civic Trust is happy to advise potential entrants on the eligibility of a particular project.

A total fund of £45,000 is available for the scheme. There is no ranking of first, second, third, etc, and no predetermined amounts for awards. However British Telecom may single out some award winning projects of 'special merit'. The value of the awards will relate to individual needs although no award will exceed £5000. (If you assume that say 20% of eligible societies enter and the average value of an award is £1000 then the chances of success are better than 1 in 5.)

The 1989 scheme allowed four months between the launch of the scheme and the 31st October deadline for entries, although this might change in future years in the light of the first year's experience. The entries are judged by assessors from British Telecom and the Civic Trust. Shortlisted entries are invited to send a representative to London to discuss their project with the assessors. (Travel expenses are paid). In late November or December, award winners are invited to a press conference in London. To ensure further local publicity cheques are presented on site by representatives of British Telecom at a point where work has started and the money needed. The information pack on the Awards includes a useful 'Project Checklist' for potential entrants.

Future: The sponsorship arrangement ensures that there will be Community Pride Awards in 1990 and 1991.

Entry: On the official entry form together with a) location plan from large-scale map, b) photographs of site, c) detailed plans and drawings, d) detailed cost estimates, e) copies of necessary consents, f) town/village guide or trail. Entrants are also encouraged to include a 'testimonial' on the community value of the awards from a leading local figure.

CO-OPERATIVE COMMUNITY AWARDS SCHEME

Education Department Co-operative Union Ltd, Stanford Hall, Loughborough, Leicestershire LE12 5QR

Telephone: 0509 852333

Contact: Peter Gormley

The scheme is organised by Co-operative Union Ltd in partnership with the Retail Co-operative Societies. The Scheme is designed 'to encourage greater participation by Co-operatives in local community development activities under the 'caring' theme'.

In 1989, twenty five awards of £100 each were offered to 'community groups or small voluntary associations who have [in the previous year] contributed to their local community or towards helping someone else'. The information on the scheme (for Retail Co-operative Societies) says that 'preference will be given to groups whose aims are primarily directed towards the general and collective community good rather than as a bi-product of another activity.

The scheme is organised as follows. Groups are nominated for awards by local Retail Co-operative Societies. Nominations (up to five from each Society) are sent to Co-operative Union Ltd and judged by a team of adjudicators under the guidance of a professional national community organiser. The critical thing as far as local community groups are concerned is to try and ensure that their group is nominated by their local Retail Co-operative Society for a national award. All this entails is submitting details of the group or organisation (name, size, aims, outstanding achievements and successes) to the relevant Retail Co-operative Society. Suggestions for nominations may be made by the group itself or by an individual unconnected with it.

Our impression is that the publicity given to this scheme varies from Society to Society. Although there is a standard leaflet (which should be stamped with the address of your local Retail Co-operative) there is no formal entry form.

Winners in 1989 included a sport and leisure club for disabled people, the Dumfries based Radio Amateur Emergency Network (which played a key role in the Lockerbie Disaster), a community shop in Warrington, a variety of health related self-help projects and a voluntary nursery for children with special needs. The majority of schemes appeared to be urban based, perhaps reflecting the commercial interests of the Retail Societies, although Co-operative Union Ltd guidelines make a point of saying that the needs of small rural communities may be more pressing than those of urban communities.

The timetable in 1989 was as follows:

Feb-April: Publicity by Societies

30th June: Deadline for suggestions to local Retail Co-operative Society

14th July: Deadline for nominations to Co-operative Union Ltd

September: Notice of successful applications to the nominating Society who arrange local publicity and presentation.

Note that the above timetable allows very little time between the deadline for local suggestions and submission of national nominations – especially relevant if more information is required. So you would be well advised to make submissions to your local Society as early as possible.

Future: The scheme has been running since 1979 and we assume will continue.

Entry: Submissions for possible national nomination must be made through local Retail Co-operative Societies.

COUNTRYSIDE CARETAKERS AWARD

Countryside Commission for Wales, Ladywell House, Newtown, Powys SY16 1RD

Telephone: 0686 626799

Sponsors: Countryside Commission for Wales and Royal Welsh Agricultural Society.

The Awards, which were instituted in 1983, are in recognition of notable achievements by the farming community in caring for the landscape and wildlife whilst producing food for the nation.

It would appear that the particular focus of the award varies from year to year. In 1989, to reflect British Food and Farming Year, the Award was for the most valuable contribution towards 'bringing about a better understanding of agriculture, food production and Welsh rural life among the public.' All working farmers in Wales are eligible to apply irrespective of the size of their farm. Entrants do not have to be members of the Royal Welsh Agricultural Society.

There is one award of £50, a specially commissioned wrought iron and copper weather vane and an illuminated certificate. Judges may commend other entrants worthy of merit. Awards are presented at the Royal Welsh Show.

Entries are submitted initially to the local Royal Welsh Agricultural Society (RWAS) Area Advisory Contact. (Addresses are included on the leaflet about the award available from the Countryside Commission for Wales – address above – and RWAS, Llanelwedd, Builth Wells, Powys, LD2 3SY, Tel: 0982 553 683). The RWAS Area Advisory Committees then visit all entrants and select one to be forwarded for assessment by the three national judges.

In 1989 entries had to be submitted by 1st May. National judging took place in June.

Future: The organisers state that the scheme will continue until 1992 but with a different focus each year.

Entry: On the official form to local RWAS contact. A plan, short report, and photographs may be included with the application.

COUNTRY LIFE FARMING AND WILDLIFE AWARD

Farming and Wildlife Trust Ltd, NAC, Stoneleigh, Kenilworth Warwickshire CV8 2RX

Telephone: 0203 696699

Contact: Jane Hampson
Sponsor: Country Life Magazine

This is an annual award scheme to find the farmer in the United Kingdom who 'has done most to encourage wildlife conservation on his farm within the constraints of successful commercial farming.' Wildlife includes fauna and flora.

Entry is open to all farmers and farm managers in the United Kingdom. Entries may be submitted jointly by farmers and landowners where conservation has been a joint endeavour. The organisers seek to ensure that small farms are given equal opportunities with large farms and arable with livestock. Each farm is judged on its merits.

The first prize is currently £1000 plus The Silver Lapwing Trophy to be held for one year and a smaller trophy to be retained. Two second prizes of £450 each are awarded. Judges may award special Certificates of Merit at their discretion.

Entries are submitted to the Secretary of the local county Farming and Wildlife Advisory Group (addresses from the Trust's address above). The county FWAG makes an initial assessment and forwards selected entries plus their own observations to the Trust. A national panel of three judges, appointed by the Editor of Country Life, then chooses a shortlist of entries to be visited and on this basis the winners are selected.

The timetable for the 1989 awards required entries to be submitted by 19th May.

Future: The Awards have been run since 1978 and are expected to continue.

Entry: On the official entry form to the local county Farming and Wildlife Advisory Group. (The entry form stipulates a maximum 250 word description of the relevant conservation work and only a sketch plan as supporting material – no other maps or photographs.)

THE DAILY TELEGRAPH AWARD

The Daily Telegraph, Marketing Department, 181 Marsh Wall, London E14

Telephone: 071 538 6264

Contact: Josie Robson
Sponsor: The Daily Telegraph

This award, first launched in 1989, is organised jointly with the

Association for Business Sponsorship of the Arts (ABSA) but is separate from the ABSA/Daily Telegraph Awards (see separate entry) which is for sponsoring businesses. The Daily Telegraph Award is for the 'individual who has contributed most to the artistic success of a sponsored [arts] activity'. 'The £5000 prize could be given to anyone contributing to the artistic success of an exhibition, a concert, opera, play or film, providing the event has been sponsored.' Nominations can be made by sponsors, arts organisations and members of the judging panel which in 1989 were John Drummond, Richard Eyre, Sir Roy Strong, Miriam Gross, and Derwent May.

The 1989 Award was launched in August with nominations required by 30th September – a rather tight timetable which presumably in future years will be more relaxed. The award was presented by the Princess of Wales in December as part of the ABSA/Daily Telegraph Awards ceremony.

Future: We have no reason to assume this Award will not continue although the organisers indicate that it might be revised.

Applications: These must be made on the official nomination form and may include two A4 pages of supplementary information plus additional material. A least one piece of material with the sponsor's name should be submitted.

THE DAILY TELEGRAPH SCHOOL NEWSPAPER COMPETITION

The Daily Telegraph, Peterborough Court at South Quay, 181 Marsh Wall, London E14 9SR

Telephone: 071 538 5000

Contact: Gabrielle Simcocks, Direct Marketing Executive
Sponsor: Daily Telegraph

This competition, in its second year in 1990, is for the best newspapers produced by children in schools (of any type) in the United Kingdom. The organisers believe that producing a newspaper 'provides an opportunity for pupils to develop a wide range of skills, from handling information and writing in different styles to problem-solving and team-work. It is also an ideal way to introduce cross-curricular subjects such as business and media studies.'

There are three age categories: 11 years and under; 12-16 years; and sixth form. The prizes are quite substantial – £1000 for first, £750 for second and £500 for third in each category. There is a £100 award for the best entry from a Special School, although Special Schools are also eligible for the main prizes in the three categories. The winning schools are invited to send three pupils to The Daily Telegraph for the day to produce a page of the paper.

The judges take account of the resources available to the school. 'Each paper will be assesed on the quality and range of its contents, the relevance of the contents to its readers, and the design and layout.' Entries may be a regular publication or a one-off edition for the competition. All entrants will be sent an assessment of their entry and a certificate according to the level reached.

The 1990 Competition, which was publicised from September 1989, required newspapers to have been produced between September 11th 1989 and February 16th 1990.

Future: We assume the competition will continue.

Entry: The 1990 competition required schools considering entering to register their interest and in return they would be sent an application form and guidelines for producing a school newspaper.

THE DISTA AWARDS FOR YOUNG PEOPLE WITH ARTHRITIS

35 Group, Arthritis Care, 5 Grosvenor Crescent, London SW1X 7ER
Telephone: 071 235 0902

Contact: Kate Nash, Director
Sponsor: Dista Products Ltd (part of Lilly Industries)

The scheme, which originated in 1981, seeks to recognise the achievements of young people, under 35, who have arthritis or some form of rheumatic disease, in community work, physical endeavour, craft and academic work. The publicity for the award quotes a previous winner as saying: 'The winning of the award is not the reason I started doing community work. But it's nice to think people you have helped think enough of you to acknowledge that help.'

Each year one winner and two runners-up are selected from each of the six regions (London and South East, East Anglia and the Midlands, South West and South Wales, North West, North Wales and Northern Ireland, North East, and Scotland). The awards are £250 for each regional winner and £75 for each of the runners-up. The awards are presented at a special luncheon in London. Entries are judged by the Medical Editorial Advisory Board of Arthritis Care.

Entry is through nomination by friends, families, organisations and professionals. The 1989 Awards required nominations to be submitted by 30th September 1989. Results were announced at the end of October.

In future years the deadline for entries will be 1st September.

During 1989 Arthritis Care organised a series of regional 'Introduction to Self-Care Courses' covering such subjects as physiotherapy and exercise management, and pain management and relaxation. The courses are promoted as part of the overall Dista Awards scheme.

Future: The Award scheme is well established and looks secure for the foreseeable future.

Entry: On the official Nomination Form. Nominators may include additional supporting information.

DOMESTOS HEALTH EDUCATION AWARDS

Domestos Health Education Awards, 50 Upper Brook Street, London W1Y 1PG

Telephone: 071 491 4568

Sponsor: Domestos (a brand of Lever Brothers Ltd)

Started in 1979 these Awards aim to recognise and reward high standards of professionalism and expertise in communication attained by health educationalists working in the community. The Awards are open to any group or individual engaged in the development and/or promotion of any aspect of health education in the United Kingdom.

Entries are also welcomed from full or part-time students on a UK course leading to a recognised UK qualification related to any aspect of health education. In the 1989 competition only projects undertaken since January 1985 were eligible.

The organisers are particularly looking for projects which 'would be of interest and value to others working in the field' and not just from 'the large health authorities and big organisations....[they] want to hear from students, smaller groups and individuals working at grass roots level. Small scale projects from health professionals are very effective and no one should feel discouraged from entering'.

In 1989 there were two categories of entry: general health education projects (first prize: £1000; second: £750; and third: £500); and AIDS related projects (first prize: £1000; and second: £500). A further £750 may be awarded for projects of outstanding merit.

The literature for the scheme provides detailed guidance for entrants. Judges look for:

- a clear statement of measurable objectives;
- appropriate methods;
- measurement and assessment of results relating to objectives;
- flair, presentation and creativity;
- conciseness.

The organisers stress the importance of 'before and after measurements' but comment that 'failure to meet objectives is by no means a bar to success....others can learn from our mistakes'

Entries are judged by an independent panel consisting of representatives from The Institute of Environmental Health, Health Visitor's Association, Institute of Health Education, Institute of Home Safety Officers, Society of Health Education Officers, Association of Community Health Councils, The Educational Sector and The Cancer Education Co-ordination Group.

Previous winners include: an interactive drama programme on drug education for 12-13 year olds; a special information leaflet for the Chinese community on AIDS; and a personal skills programme designed to improve the self-image of maladjusted 11-16 year old boys.

The timetable for the 1989 Awards required entries to be submitted by 20th October 1989. Winners were due to be notified in December and presented with their awards in January 1990.

Future: A well-established scheme that seems likely to continue.

Entry: On the official entry form, which requires a very brief synopsis of the project, together with a fairly detailed submission structured according the 'Guidelines for Entrants'.

THE DRAGON AWARDS

Business in the Community, 227a City Road, London, EC1V 1LX
Telephone: 071 253 3716 (BT Hotline: 071 608 3228)

Contact: Lesley Harvey
Sponsor/co-organiser: Corporation of London

The Dragon Awards are given to firms and institutions based in the City of London or a London Borough in recognition of significant contributions to the improvement of community life and employment opportunities. Applicants must be either a business of any size in the private sector, a nationalised industry, a livery company, corporate trust or foundation. As an objective of the Awards is to promote the wider recognition of good ideas, firms and institutions are encouraged to nominate themselves.

In 1989 the following broad categories were adopted:

• Young City ... activities undertaken by young people in the City involving raising funds or providing advice and assistance to community projects.

• City Opportunities ... provision of training and work-experience for school-leavers especially those who experience unemployment or disadvantage.

• City Enterprise ... support for the development of small enterprises in areas of inner city stress or high unemployment.

• Community Investment ... provision of loans and other investment assistance for urban rgeneration projects.

• Community Service ... organisation of schemes and events in which employees and the business provide free help for charitable and voluntary activities of benefit to the community.

Sponsorship of sport, recreation or the arts is not eligible.

Although five awards, of a small replica of the dragon marking the City boundaries, were made by the judges in 1989, they were not bound to make an award in each of the above categories. Judges pay particular attention to: the number of people who benefit; the promotion of opportunities for employment and community life; projects which promote a better understanding of the role of the City as a business centre; originality; and the potential for replication elsewhere. Initiatives from all sizes of firms and institutions will be considered. The initiative need not be based in London – indeed 'the judges are particularly seeking examples of London resources benefitting the regions as a response to the North/South divide'.

Although these awards are given to firms and other institutions it may well be worthwhile for charities and groups 'on the receiving end' of support from City-based organisations to encourage their corporate supporters to enter the competition. Indeed the organisers actively encourage this. The publicity spin-offs could be valuable. In 1988 The Financial Times published a feature on the award winners and the organisers themselves published a booklet describing all 60 entries in the 1989 competition. A concert and reception was organised to celebrate the Awards in 1989.

Detailed Guidelines for applicants are available from the organisers. For the 1989 Awards initiatives had to be started, completed or in existence throughout the period 1st April 1988 to 31st March 1989. Nominations had to be submitted by 31st March 1989

Future: We assume this scheme will continue, although the broad categories may vary from year to year.

Entry: On the official nomination form, submitted by the firm or institution responsible for the initiative. Supporting material may be included.

THE DUCHY OF CORNWALL DEVON YOUNG FARMERS CLUBS COUNTRYSIDE PROJECT

Devon Federation of Young Farmers' Clubs, Amory Building, The Cattle Market, Marsh Barton Road, Exeter, Devon EX2 8LH
Telephone: 0392 72189

Contact: Sue Eberle
Sponsor: The Duchy of Cornwall

The aim of this award is to encourage Young Farmers throughout Devon to become involved in projects that incorporate conservation principles in the widest sense into farming and land management operations. It is designed to widen people's perceptions of conservation to incorporate such subjects as buildings, the rural community, archaeology, rural skills as well as wildlife conservation and to encourage them to take particular action to conserve their local heritage. All clubs in the Devon Federation of Young Farmers Clubs are eligible to enter the competition. (Remember you do not have to be involved in farming to be a member of a Young Farmers Club.)

For the initial judging the county is divided into four areas with a winner from each selected to take part in the overall county competition. Trophies are awarded to the county and area winners and certificates presented to all participating clubs which make a 'reasonable effort at a sensible project'. Presentations are made at the Devon County Show in May.

The organisers state that entries 'must have some lasting benefit to the natural or manmade environment and the people who live there'. They may embrace any aspect of environmental and heritage conservation. Particular emphasis is placed on the planning stage of projects and the seeking of professional advice prior to commencing a project. Judges take into account the size of the club and the commitment of its members to the competition when assessing entries.

The competition is intended to be an annual event which will commence in September with judging in the following April. Entries in the 1989 competition had to be submitted by 29th September.

Future: The organisers clearly intend the competition to be an annual event.

Entry: In 1989, the organisers arranged four area meetings to introduce the competition. This was followed by two further meetings at which participating clubs were invited to present their proposed projects to a panel of experts who advised entrants on the need for and sources of further advice and expertise. We are not aware of a special application form although full details are available from the above address.

DULUX COMMUNITY PROJECTS

Welbeck Golin/Harris, 43 King Street, Covent Garden, London WC2E 8RJ
Telephone: 071 836 6677

Contact: Alison Sellman
Sponsor: ICI Paints

This is a two-stage scheme managed for ICI Paints, the manufacturers of Dulux, by a public relations agency. The first stage involves the donation of (in 1989) £60,000 worth of paint to voluntary groups and community projects. An independent Selection Panel decides which of the projects merits donations of paint and then allocates supplies accordingly. The Selection Panel includes representatives from both the National Council for Voluntary Organisations and the Civic Trust.

The second stage involves cash awards – the Special Selection. Literature for the scheme states: ' the Selection Panel will select twenty projects (four from each of five geographical areas) which they consider may merit a further cash award by reason of offering the greatest potential in terms of creativity and benefit to the community.' 'Allocation of the cash awards will be based on 'before and after' photography organised by the Dulux Community Projects office, and on the originality and worthiness of the individual projects – supported, if necessary, by a site visit.' A total of £7000 was available for cash awards in 1989, but the value of individual awards will 'be determined at the sole discretion of the Selection Panel.' Cash award winners are invited to attend a presentation in London which also includes a photographic exhibition of their work.

The five areas from which award winners are selected are: 1) Scotland and Northern Ireland; 2) East Midlands and North East England; 3) Mid and North Wales, West Midlands and North West England; 4) Central Southern England, East Anglia and London; 5) South East, Southern and South West England and South Wales.

The Scheme is open to: 'any non-profit making bona-fide voluntary group, registered charity, club, school or similar organisation.'

In 1989 projects receiving donations of paint (and cash awards) included an adventure playground in Chester, a mural on a pre-cast stone wall in Newcastle, and repainting of stables used by a Riding for the Disabled project. In general, a donation of 30 litres of paint is considered small, 150 litres average, and 500 litres large.

In 1989 the timetable for the scheme was as follows:

26th May: Closing date for applications

30th July: Notification of paint donations to successful applicants. Notification of projects shortlisted for Special Selection Cash Awards

15th September: Completion of painting by Special Selection projects

October: Announcement of cash awards.

Future: This is a well established scheme which seems likely to continue in a similar form in future years. Application forms for the scheme are normally available in the Spring, and that there might be some changes in the detail of the scheme from year to year.

Entry: Applications must be made on the official form which requires a description of the proposed painting project and a specific and accurate statement of the quantity, type and colour of paint required. Remember that to be eligible for Special Selection Awards painting work will have to be completed between 30th July and 15th September (in 1989). (Groups awarded paint but not invited to join the Special Selection can paint to their own timescale.)

(COUNTY) DURHAM ENVIRONMENT AWARD

Environment Department, Durham County Council, County Hall, Durham DH1 5UQ

Telephone: 091 386 4411.

Contact: Director of Environment

The objective of this award scheme is to encourage good design in all aspects of the built and natural environment and to promote the care of the environment through sensitive schemes that conserve and enhance natural features and demonstrate good guardianship.

To be eligible, projects must improve the environment of County Durham – the scheme leaflet gives some illustrations. These include: new buildings or extensions and conversions that enhance the townscape of an area or paving schemes that improve the street scene, tree planting, stone wall building, nature conservation projects, landscaping, anti-pollution schemes by voluntary or statutory bodies and 'environmentally friendly' industrial processes.

The scheme is open to anyone, including individuals, community groups, amenity societies, schools and companies. In the 1989 competition projects should have been substantially undertaken during the year 1st April 1989 to 31st March 1990. A plaque, certificate and unspecified 'modest' financial prize are awarded to outstanding submissions.

The deadline for submissions to the 1989 competition was 31st December. Awards were presented during Environment Week at the end of April 1990.

Future: We assume the competition is intended to be an annual event.

Entry: On the simple entry form/information leaflet together with photographs or drawings to illustrate the project.

ETHA – EDUCATION THROUGH HERITAGE AND THE ARTS

Heritage Education Trust, St Mary's College, Strawberry Hill, Twickenham TW1 4SX

Telephone: 081 892 0051 ext 202

Contact: Martin Dyer, Chief Executive
Sponsor: The Headley Trust

This new project, launched at the end of 1989, is designed 'to encourage schools throughout the country to turn to the resources of the heritage for inspiration, to develop their own creative ideas therefrom, and to present their findings in a form which will entertain an audience, using whichever expressive skills they choose'. The organisers see the project as presenting 'new opportunities for (heritage) property owners and administrators to co-operate with schools to make educational visits an integral and on-going part of the curriculum'.

Participating schools are invited to do two things:

1. Stage a performance of one of a cycle of three cantatas specially commissioned for the project. All three cantatas will be composed by Michael Hurd and will 'tell a story of British History'. The first to be completed, The Liberty Tree, is inspired by aspects of the English Civil War of 1642-1660.

2. Select an aspect or aspects of the heritage inspired by the chosen cantata and present it in their own original way. This could include music, creative historical writing, a dramatic presentation, painting, graphic design, costume design, video, audio tape, etc, or a combination of two or more offerings which can be either collective or from individuals.

The project will culminate in a concert and presentation by finalist schools in 1991.

Further details of the project which were not available at the time of writing can be obtained from the organisers. By December 1989 the organisers had received requests for further information from over 350 schools.

EDWARD MORSHEAD AWARD

Dartmoor National Park, Headquarters, Parke, Bovey Tracey, Newton Abbot, Devon TQ13 9JQ
Telephone: 0626 832093

Contact: Information Officer
Sponsor: No sponsor confirmed but sponsorship being pursued.

In September 1989 the Dartmoor National Park Committee resolved to institute an annual award in memory of Edward Morshead who had contributed much to environmental conservation in the National Park and Devon as a whole.

The award is intended to recognise and motivate contributions to the purposes of the national park by individuals and voluntary organisations. It is suggested that the award should be open to residents of Dartmoor and those individuals and bodies based near enough to it to be regular users of the National Park.

The award is for work relating to landscape conservation (in its broadest sense). The following activities are cited as examples of possible entries: rehabilitation of a building in the public eye, restoration of walls, hedgebanks or gateways, woodland management, high quality stockmanship and the maintenance of moorland and farmland views.

The award itself takes the form of a trophy (a sculpted Dartmoor pony) and a cash prize.

Entry: Anyone who wishes to receive information when it is available should register their interest with the Dartmoor National Park.

ELMBRIDGE COMMUNITY CLEAN UP PRIZE

Public Relations Department, Elmbridge Borough Council, Elmbridge Town Hall, New Zealand Avenue, Walton-on-Thames, KT12 1PS

Telephone: 0932 228844

Contact: Public Relations Officer
Sponsor: Air Products

In 1989 Elmbridge Borough Council organised, for the first time, 'Community Clean-Up Week', an initiative designed to encourage action to improve the environment of the Borough. In 1989 the week was 10th to 17th September. Local groups were invited to choose a project or projects 'which will spruce up the borough' and submit these to the Borough Council. The scheme's information leaflet gives examples of creating a wildlife sanctuary, clearing a neglected pond, tree planting and getting rid of a local eyesore as potential entries.

An award is presented by the Mayor of Elmbridge for 'the most effective community project'. In 1989 the presentation took place on 17th September at the Walton Country Weekend.

The organisers try to ensure that a particular project is not chosen by more than one group but we have no further information on the judging criteria, timetable or other arrangements.

Future: We understand that the 1989 scheme was successful which suggests that it may well be repeated in subsequent years.

Entry: On the official and simple entry form.

ENVIRONMENTAL ENTERPRISE AWARD

World Wide Fund for Nature – United Kingdom (WWF-UK), Panda House, Weyside Park, Godalming, Surrey, GU7 1XR

Telephone: 0483 426444

Contact: Peter Martin
Sponsors: Department of Education and Science and The Laura Ashley Foundation

This new scheme, for schools and colleges, was announced in January 1989. The award is designed to encourage young people to identify an environmental issue that concerns them and, by using their ingenuity and skills and seeking outside advice where needed, to produce practical solutions to problems or enhance the environment in some way. The scheme is intended to support the aims and objectives of the National Curriculum, especially in the fields of design and technology and science.

The competition is part of a major programme, costing some £120,000 per year, to develop links between environmental education and science and design and technology. The programme involves the provision of back-up material, some of it produced by specialist organisations such as Intermediate Technology Group, teachers courses in partnership with the Science and Technology Regional Organisations, a publication drawing on practical classroom experience and the appointment at WWF-UK of a full-time officer to co-ordinate the programme and promote networking.

The scheme leaflet gives examples of designing a solar powered water pump, constructing a compost maker for the school kitchen, or protecting an area of countryside from erosion as possible entries. It states: 'the range of possibilities can be wide and need not necessarily be tied in to your local environment. We are inviting teachers to help young people to develop an awareness of the link between their classroom learning, the environment and industry, by involving them in specific projects that have captured their imagination.' It is hoped that entrants will be able to interest firms, public authorities and organisations with environmental responsibilities in their projects and that these bodies might take up the ideas afterwards. Over 1600 schools and colleges had registered their interest in the Awards as at 31st October 1989 – which the organisers view as a very encouraging response.

Entry is open to all schools in England and Wales and to pupils under 19 years of age (on 31st August 1990) attending further education or tertiary colleges. There are three categories of entry as follows (age as on 31st August 1990):

A: Individual pupils or groups of up to 10 pupils aged 17-19;
First prize: £4000; Second prize: £2000; Third prize: £1000

B: Individual pupils or groups of up to 10 pupils aged 12-16;
First prize: £2000; Second prize: £1000; Third prize: £600

C: Any group of pupils aged 7-11;
First prize: £1000; Second prize: £800; Third prize: £400

Awards are made to the school or college and not the individuals. Runners-up in each category will receive commendations.

In the first instance judging will involve a scrutiny of final reports. At later stages candidates may be asked to submit or demonstrate further practical evidence of their projects. The judging panel will include business people, teachers, scientists, engineers, environmentalists and technologists.

The scheme was launched in July 1989, schools were invited to register their interest up to the end of 1989 and submit final presentations by the end of the Spring Term 1990. (See below for details of entry procedure)

Future: Funding is committed for a three-year programme and a competition will be run in each of these years. It is possible that in each year the competition will focus on a particular theme, such as energy conservation or recycling.

Entry: There are three stages in the entry process:

1. Entrants register their interest (using the coupon on the information leaflet) and in return receive an Award Fact File.

2. The Award Fact File contains a progress report form which must be returned by January 1990. This enables the organisers to record basic details of the project and entrants.

3. Final presentations, in the form of an A4 report, should be submitted by the end of the Spring Term 1990. This should be a fairly detailed report and be submitted with photographs, drawings and

plans if appropriate. Entrants also need to describe how the award money would be used.

ENVIRONMENT WEEK AWARDS

A large number of local civic and amenity societies launched new competitions and award schemes to take place in Environment Week (normally end of April/beginning of May) to mark European Year of the Environment in 1988. Many of these have now become established on a regular annual basis. However we have only been able to obtain information, often of a limited nature, on relatively few. These are simply listed below. The Civic Trust (17 Carlton House Terrace, London SW1Y 5AW, Tel: 071 930 0914) with which the majority of societies and Environment Week activities are registered may be able to advise on schemes operating within specific geographical areas.

Bridgwater and District Civic Society – Environmental Enhancement Awards: 15 Quantock Avenue, Bridgwater, Somerset, TAM6 7EB. *Contact:* C N Hill, Honorary Secretary

Felixstowe Society – competition for schools: 44 Brook Lane, Felixstowe, Suffolk, IP11 7JP. *Contact:* Barbara Reed, Secretary

Llanelli Civic Society – competition for schools and youth groups: 36 Queen Victoria Road, Llanelli, Dyfed, SA15 2TH Tel: 0554 758891 *Contact:* Brynmor Voyle

Pembroke Civic Trust Society – theme undecided: 19 Paynter Street, Pembroke SA71 4ED Tel: 0646 682520. *Contact:* Mrs M Price, Secretary

ETHNIC MINORITIES AWARD SCHEME (EMAS)

c/o Inner Cities Unit, NCVO, 26 Bedford Square, London, WC1B 3HU
Telephone: 071 636 4066

Contact: Judy Ling Wong
Sponsors: Countryside Commission, UK2000, MediaNatura, Rayne Foundation, Callhaven plc, Anderson Fraser and NCVO.

EMAS is an independent project based at NCVO run by a steering group of people with diverse backgrounds and coordinated by Judy Ling Wong who herself won an award in 1987.

EMAS aims to encourage environmental projects undertaken by members of ethnic minority groups. The EMAS booklet, 'Opening up the Environment' states that '... traditionally, environmental care and celebration have been the domain of a narrow section of society. EMAS aims to challenge this, by creating a climate in which environmental care and celebration include the missing contribution of ethnic minority groups.'

EMAS provides advice, information and development support and runs a small grants scheme to help make projects happen. Although not a competition, in the sense of awarding completed projects, we nevertheless felt that it would be appropriate to include details of the scheme in this book.

Projects eligible for grants should be ethnic minority managed and involve a significant number (though not necessarily a majority) of participants from ethnic minorities. New projects will have priority over established ones and projects without significant established funding will have priority over ones that do. All types of environmental projects are eligible. There are special caategories for school and youth club projects.

The maximum grant is £1000 but the majority of grants are likely to range from £50 to £500. However, the organisers of the Scheme are quite prepared to consider further support in future years. As they state: 'One project started off with a £250 EMAS grant last year and ended up with £2650 plus a lot of extra assistance on top of that in expertise and volunteer help.'

EMAS does have project categories: projects/events/outings to promote use of green spaces in inner cities; improvement schemes; exhibitions; conferences; play events; competitions; allotments and food-growing; projects which release potential through encouraging positive attitudes to the environemnt; festivals; and 'anything else'. Clearly the Scheme is very wide-ranging and flexible.

Winning projects in 1987 included planting boxes outside a Mosque and Islamic Cultural Centre in Sheffield, a street mural in Birmingham, countryside outings organised by the Muslim Disabled Association in Batley, Yorkshire and a cultural garden at a school in Lambeth.

For the 1989 Scheme completed applications had to be submitted by 31st January 1990 with grants awarded by March 1990.

Future: We assume the Scheme will continue.

Entry: On the official application form.

EUROPA NOSTRA AWARDS

Secretariat, Europa Nostra Awards, 9 Buckingham Gate, London SW1E 6JP

Telephone: 071 821 1171

Contact: Marianne Malonne, Deputy Secretary General
Sponsor: American Express

Europa Nostra, founded in 1963, is a European federation of associations whose aim is to protect Europe's cultural and natural heritage and to improve the environment. One of its activities is the organisation of the annual Europa Nostra Awards for projects which make a distinguished contribution to the conservation and enhancement of Europe's architectural and natural heritage.

Europa Nostra currently embraces organisations in the following countries: Austria, Belgium, Cyprus, Denmark, Finland, France, West Germany, Greece, Ireland, Italy, Luxembourg, Malta, Netherlands, Norway, Portugal, Spain, Sweden, Switzerland, Turkey and the United Kingdom. However this does not appear to preclude entries for the awards from outside these countries. (Hungary had a winner in 1988).

The following types of projects may be entered:
- restoration of old buildings;
- adaptation of old buildings for new uses, preserving their original character;
- conservation of natural or historic landscapes;
- new construction in conservation areas, harmonising sympathetically with the older environment, or which pays due respect to the environment in areas of outstanding natural beauty.

Projects must have been completed within ten years prior to entry.

All winners (over 40 in number) receive a plaque for mounting on their building and a diploma. Up to seven winners may be specially recognised with the award of a silver medal and further special awards may also be made. Entries are judged by the International Executive Committee of Europa Nostra.

Entries may be submitted, by owners, occupiers, architects or designers, under one of the following categories of client organisation responsible for commissioning the work:

- private owners
- civic or amenity societies
- commercial owners
- regional or local government
- national government

The 1988 winners, documented in the information for the 1989 awards, were, with one exception (a Maltese nature reserve), all concerned with the built environment, either the restoration or construction of a single building or the rehabilitation of an area of a town or city (major inner city projects in Glasgow and Antwerp were among the eight medal winners). A breakdown of 1988 winners by the type of organisation commissioning the work reveals the following: eight private projects, eight civic/amenity society projects, two commercial projects (both from the UK), seventeen local/regional government projects, nine national government projects and one joint civic society/local government project.

The timetable for the 1989 Awards required entries to be submitted by 20th October 1989. Winners were due to be notified in mid-January 1990 and other entrants notified in the spring of 1990.

Future: A very well established scheme which we assume will continue for some time.

Entry: On the official entry form together with a history and description of the project (max 1000 words), 'before and after' photographs and other supporting material presented in a hard backed A4 folder or ring binder.

EYEBRIGHT

The Association for the Protection of Rural Scotland, 14a Napier Road Edinburgh EH10 5AY

Telephone: 031 229 1081

Contact: Robert L Smith, Director
Sponsor: Calor Gas Scotland

The purpose of this scheme is to encourage good rehabilitation of derelict areas and to recognise particularly fine examples of such work in a rural setting. Each project is to be seen as making a definite contribution to its own neighbourhood. Projects located outside of major conurbations are eligible as are those in Green Belt areas of conurbations. All projects must be in Scotland.

APRS also run an Eyebright Junior Award, for children in Strathclyde Region, and an annual Award for new buildings and structures (in even years) and reconstruction of buildings and structures (in odd years). These are covered in separate entries in this book.

The organisers of Eyebright give examples of the type of projects eligible for an award. They include: rehabilitation of land after mining, quarrying, rubbish dumping or other industrial use; rehabilitation and creation of paths, cycle ways and horse rides on derelict railway lines and canal banks; farm landscaping; and restoration of a village green or monument. This list is by no means comprehensive. Rehabilitation of individual or groups of buildings are excluded unless part of a broader rehabilitation scheme. (They may be eligible for the Annual APRS Award referred to above). Projects will be judged in categories according to: the size and scale of the project; the sources and amount of funding; and the originality and innovative nature of the project.

Submissions or nominations may be made by any individual, firm, organisation, community council, local or central government authority. All entrants will be visited by a local panel of judges who will submit their selections to the main panel who will undertake further visits in late spring and early summer. Awards will be presented in Glasgow in September. The overall winner receives a specially designed trophy, and a certificate. In 1988 eighteen finalists each received a certificate and silver-plated miniature Calor gas cylinder.

Projects must have been completed by 30th December 1989 and entries submitted by the end of January 1990 in the case of the 1990 Eyebright Award.

Future: The 1990 Eyebright competition was the second, and both sponsors and organisers are keen to continue the scheme.

Entry: On the official entry form with the following material:

a) up to six photographs illustrating the project ('before' photographs would also be helpful);

b) a brief description to a maximum of 400 words;

c) an Ordnance Survey reference and clear site plan.

EYEBRIGHT JUNIOR

The Association for the Protection of Rural Scotland, 1, Craigbrae Cottages, Drongan, Ayr KA6 7EN

Telephone: 0292 590273

Contact: Rob Close
Sponsors: Calor Gas Scotland/Strathclyde Regional Council

(Note that the address above is for Mr Close, the administrator of the competition, and not APRS headquarters which is: 14a Napier Road, Edinburgh, EH10 5AY.)

This award is to encourage children in rural areas of Strathclyde to improve, or plan how to improve, derelict, neglected or untidy areas of ground in the countryside near their schools. Schemes are expected to make a positive contribution to the local environment. Examples of eligible projects are: tidying up areas used as unofficial litter dumps; restoring a village green or monument; converting land into a garden or playground; and revealing and making accessible relics of early industry. This list is by no means comprehensive.

Entries must be submitted through the school. There are two categories of entry: 'design only' projects where children develop concepts and ideas for ways in which areas may be improved; and 'practical work' projects. The latter must have been started within the two years prior to the deadline for submissions, which in the case of the 1990 Awards is 31st May. Entries are judged in two sections – for Primary levels 5, 6 and 7 and Secondary levels 3 and 4. The winning entry in each category receives a plaque, the overall winner receives a 'special prize' and there are other 'rewards as appropriate'.

Future: This is a pilot project which if successful will lead to a competition in 1991/92 for all rural schools in Scotland.

Entry: On the official entry/nomination form together with:

a) drawings or photographs;

b) suggestions for improvements illustrated by plans etc and description of how these could be achieved – including cost and funding ('design only');

c) description of work undertaken, cost, and funding ('practical projects');

d) Ordnance Survey reference and site plan.

FORD CONSERVATION AWARDS

The Conservation Foundation, 1 Kensington Gore, London SW7 2AR
Telephone: 071 823 8842

Contact: None given
Sponsor: Ford Motor Company Ltd

The Awards, which have been run since 1982, aim to encourage conservation initiatives in a wide range of categories by public and community groups. There are at present four categories of Entry:

Natural environment: Projects aimed at conserving flora, fauna and their respective habitats. Entries might include wildlife reserves, coastline improvement or woodland management.

Young people's projects: Any conservation project undertaken individually or collectively by anyone of 18 years and under. Work may have been under adult guidance but must have been carried out by young people.

Heritage: Projects designed to conserve man-made aspects of British heritage, including conservation of folk traditions, old buildings, crafts or modes of transport.

Conservation engineering: Projects designed to reduce the rate of consumption of finite resources, or to reduce pollution using new technology, or new applications for old technology. Schemes which can show a measurable improvement will stand the best chance.

There is a trophy and a £2500 prize for each category winner and a trophy and £5000 prize for the overall UK Winner which is designated the 'National Conservation Project of the Year'. The overall UK winner is also submitted into the Ford European Conservation Award finals which embrace thirteen countries.

The key criteria used by judges in both the UK and European Awards are:

1. Does the project address a real need for conservation?

2. Effort, enthusiasm and skill by those involved.

3. Originality in approach – a new way of tackling an old problem or a solution to a new problem?

4. The benefit of winning an award.

5. Any European dimension – could the project be implemented on a European scale.

However the organisers do not expect entries to meet all these criteria and wish to encourage entries even if they appear deficient in any of the above.

The overall UK winner in 1989 was The Rare Breeds Survival Trust. Other winners were Scottish Conservation Projects' Footpath Management Scheme, Caroline Fawcett's Lincolnshire Nature Reserve and The Palm House at Kew Gardens. European winners in 1988 included the Swiss town of Onex for a new network of urban hedgerows, the Diepenbeek arboretum in Belgium and, the European winner, a German project which has created a series of protected wetland reserves for indigenous and migratory birds.

In 1989 the deadline for entries was 1st September and the awards were presented at a ceremony at The Mansion House on November 3rd. The European Final was held in Cologne in December.

Future: The Ford Conservation Awards are well established and seem likely to continue.

Entry: On the official entry form available from The Conservation Foundation.

GATEWAY INTERPRET BRITAIN AWARD

The Society for the Interpretation of Britain's Heritage c/o 4 Holmewood Close, Kenilworth, Warwickshire CV8 2JE

Contact: Ian Parkin, Awards Organiser
Sponsor: Gateway Foodmarkets Ltd

Note that the main office address for SIBH is: c/o Centre for Environmental Interpretation, Bellhouse Building, Lower Ormond Street, Manchester M15 6BX (Telephone: 061 228 6171 ext 2540).

(See also a separate entry on the related VPB Design Award for Interpretive Panels.)

The purpose of this award scheme is to recognise and publicise outstanding practice in the provision of interpretive facilities for visitors throughout the United Kingdom (which in this case includes Orkney and Shetland, the Isle of Man and the Channel Islands). It is open to any organisation in the public, private or voluntary sectors which presents interpretation of a place, site or facility for the benefit of the public.

The following interpretive media are eligible: exhibitions, displays, ranger services, guides, on-site interpretation, living history using drama or events, visitor and heritage centres and specific publications (excluding newspapers, magazines, articles and broadcasts). To be eligible the scheme must have been open or available to the public during the majority of the previous visitor season. The project must be complete and in the case of walks and events be continuing in the summer of the year of entry.

Award winners receive a mounted plaque and commended schemes receive a framed certificate. There may be a special award in any year – in 1989, thanks to support from UK2000, this was for projects wholly or substantially implemented through MSC/Training Agency programmes.

There are no formal categories but the following points should be noted:

• schemes must be open to the public.

• schemes are judged primarily on the interpretive content (themes, media, quality of presentation, effectiveness of communication, attitude of staff) although ancillary facilities and services are taken into account.

- schemes should show appropriate involvement of the local community and volunteers, and show adequate provision for disabled people.

- discrete parts of overall schemes must be capable of assessment in their own right.

- entries which consist of a first phase or part of a larger scheme must state the full extent of the scheme and the relationship of the entered part with the whole.

In 1989 entries had to be submitted by 13th May 1989. Awards were presented by Magnus Magnusson in Glasgow on 18th January 1990 in conjunction with a conference on 'Interpretation, Culture and the Arts'. The organisers normally expect to announce and present the awards within one calendar year of the competition.

The judging procedure is as follows. Initial evaluation is undertaken by an Assessor nominated by SIBH on the basis of the application form and supporting material. The Assessors visit shortlisted schemes and make recommendations to a national Awards Panel of recognised experts, who are responsible for determining the winners.

Notes on the award winning and commended projects are prepared each year and these are published in looseleaf form to build up a continually expanding 'Manual of Good Practice'. (These are available from the above address.) Previous winners have included museums, guided walks, trails, events programmes, heritage centres, books, the preparation of interpretive strategies.

Future: The organisers are committed to continuing the scheme in future years although this is dependent on securing sponsorship. At the time of writing, Gateway had not confirmed its intentions for 1990 and beyond although the organisers were optimistic that the association would continue.

Entry: On the official entry form with a location plan, supporting documentation and up to six black and white photographs (A5) and six 35mm colour slides.

THE GLENFIDDICH LIVING SCOTLAND AWARD

Applications should be made to: The Glenfiddich Distillery, Dufftown Banffshire AB5 4DH
Telephone: 0340 20373

Contact: Jean McLeod

Information also available from: Tait and McLay Advertising, 9 Royal Crescent, Glasgow G3 7SP, Contact: David M Tait, Secretary to Judges, Glenfiddich Awards. Telephone 041 332 0193.

Sponsor: William Grant & Sons Ltd (distillers of Glenfiddich Malt whisky)

This Award Scheme is designed 'to promote and conserve Scotland's heritage and traditions in the widest sense, whether it be in the context of the natural environment, or of human history, culture and achievement'. Projects may be of a practical character, conserving aspects of particular heritage value, or they may be of an academic or educational nature, involving an element of research, aimed at achieving a better understanding of their importance.

It is important to note that the Awards are usually for projects planned but not yet implemented although they may occasionally be made to supplement the funding of schemes already in progress, but rarely for work already completed. This is therefore more akin to a grant scheme to stimulate activity than a competition to recognise achievement. Applications may be submitted at any time. The size and number of awards are not specified, varying according to the needs of the individual applicants. The organisers state that it is rare for more than £6000 to be allocated to a single project.

Applications are inspected by the judges or their appointed assessors with special emphasis being placed on 'the value of each project to their community and their contribution to a better understanding of the importance of conservation in Scotland today'. A shortlist is then drawn up for final review by the panel of four judges which is headed by the Marquess of Bute. The final decision is usually taken in mid-summer.

Projects funded over the five years of the scheme to date include the establishment of an otter haven in Deeside, the restoration of one of Scotland's oldest railway wagons, research into the life of Scots opera star Joseph Hislop, the setting-up of an ornamental plasterwork museum in Peebles, a photographic survey of Mull, an artist funded to produce a series on 'The Oil Worker in Scotland' and underwater archaoelogical excavations in Loch Tay.

Future: The organisers state that the scheme will continue for the forseeable future.

Entry: On the official entry form (which requires the names and addresses of two referees) plus, where appropriate, a separate description of the project of up to 1000 words, together with relevant diagrams, photographs or maps.

GLOUCESTERSHIRE FOOTPATH HERITAGE COMPETITION

Gloucestershire Area, The Ramblers' Association, 6 Elm Lodge, Woodleigh, 65 The Park, Cheltenham, GL50 2RY

Telephone: 0242 515786

Contact: Joan Kelland, Area Secretary

This competition is for parish and town councils in Gloucestershire. It is designed to stimulate local pride in the footpath network.

The organisers see the competition as a means of encouraging and recognising action to improve the physical state of footpaths and to promote their use by local people and visitors from near and far.

'The competition is not to find the council with the best kept paths but to find the council which has done the most to improve its paths during the previous two years.'

The competition is run every two years — with a special emphasis each year. The 1990 competition looked especially for councils which had been successful in securing the observance of 'the ploughing code' — a code of practice for farmers in respect of cross field paths. 'Councils which liaise with farmers and secure compliance with the code will be particularly favourably considered in the judging.'

In general, entries may cover physical improvement schemes, parish walks, local walks leaflets, and publicly displayed parish maps as well as any other activity or programme in furtherance of the competition's objectives.

The award, The Footpath Heritage Trophy, is an impressive ironwork sculpture for outdoor display made by a Gloucestershire craftsman. The Trophy is passed on from winner to winner. Judging is based on the 'claims for improvements' submitted by entrants.

The 1990 competition required entries to be submitted by 31st January 1990, but the organisers stressed the importance of councils undertaking survey work and identifying particular problems during the preceeding summer and autumn. Claims for improvements had to be submitted by 31st July 1990.

Future: We understand that the competition has not, so far, attracted the level of interest the organisers would like, although we have no reason to suggest that the scheme will not continue.

Entry: Initially on the official entry form followed by submission of a 'claims for improvement' form describing the work/activities undertaken. There is an entry fee of £4.

THE GRAHAM ALLEN AWARD FOR CONSERVATION

Planning Department, North Norfolk District Council, PO Box 5, Cromer Norfolk NR27 9DZ

Telephone: 0263 513811 ext. 4292

Contact: Mr Hudson

An annual award, in memory of the first Chairman of the District Council, for the scheme which makes the most successful contribution to the conservation of the environment of North Norfolk district. The Award is open to conservation schemes involving the built environment or the countryside irrespective of scale. Entries may be submitted by owners, clients, architects, designers, contractors and manufacturers. There is no limit to the number of entries from any one source although the prior approval of the owner/occupier must be obtained.

The main award is a plaque suitable for permanent external display. 'Highly Commended' and 'Commended' projects may also be awarded a certificate. The award winners are selected by a panel of judges nominated by the Development Committee of the District Council.

Entries must be submitted by 30th June and must relate to schemes completed after 1st January of the previous year.

Future: This is an annual award which we assume will continue.

Entry: On the official entry form together with photographs - preferably illustrating the scheme both before and after work was undertaken.

GREAT ENVELOPE COMPETITION

Organiser: DRG Stationery Products, Apsley, Hemel Hempstead, Herts HP3 9SS

Telephone: 0442 421244

For further information on the competition contact: Group Public Relations PLC, 5 Langley Street, London WC2H 9JA. Telephone: 071 379 3404. Contact: Julie Todd.

Sponsors: Direct Response Magazine/Royal Mail

The competition is designed to recognise and promote creativity and cost-effectiveness in the design of direct mail envelopes. Direct Mail is an increasingly sophisticated 'tool' used by charities for promotion and fundraising. Although these awards are focussed on design and thus on the direct marketing agency rather than the client, the publicity associated with an award will no doubt benefit the charity concerned. Also it might be reasonable to suggest that a cash prize relating to a charity campaign be donated to that charity!

Entry is free and open to any UK company, charity or agency. The organisers stress that entries do not have to be part of a huge print run – they are looking for 'big ideas not big budgets'. The 1989 competition had three main categories: best business-to-business envelope, best consumer envelope and best charity envelope – the last a new category for 1989. The winner in each category received a cash prize of £250. In addition there was a prize for the overall 'Best Design' (£1000) and a £250 prize for the best envelope by a young designer (in their first year of full-time employment as a graphic designer). Other entries worthy of particular recognition received commendations.

Judging is on the basis of creativity, cost effectiveness and relevance to the promotion. Creativity is given special importance. In 1989 the judges included representatives of the sponsors, a major national charity and leading direct marketing agencies. (Being one of the judges does not appear to preclude your agency from submitting an entry.)

The deadline for entries in the 1989 competition was Friday 14th July 1989. Winners were presented with their awards at a special luncheon in late September and featured in the October issue of Direct Response Magazine.

Future: We assume this competition will continue.

Entry: On the official entry form together with six samples of each entry. A design may be submitted for more than one category. Entrants may submit as many designs as they wish – as long as a separate form (photocopied if necessary) is submitted for each design.

GREEN CON OF THE YEAR AWARD

Friends of the Earth, 26-28 Underwood Street, London N1 7JQ
Telephone: 071 490 1555

Contact: None given

Probably the only competition in this book which nominees would prefer not to win. Friends of the Earth launched this 'award' on Green Shopping Day – 28th September 1989. The Award was a response to the increasing trend of companies to promote themselves as 'environmentally friendly' while continuing to be involved in processes, activities and products which damage the environment. Friends of the Earth, concerned at the false or misleading claims made by companies, saw the Award as a means of drawing attention to such practices.

At the time of writing little information about the award, which had arisen spontaneously from FoE's Annual Conference earlier in the year, was available. The nature of the award had not been decided, nor had any formal judging criteria although it is intended that criteria would be developed for the 1990 award in the light of the first year's experience. However, in their letter to local group co-ordinators in October 1989 inviting nominations FoE indicated that the categories of obvious concern were:

- misleading advertising or PR copy;
- industry claiming a green image when the reality was very different;
- companies claiming things are environmentally friendly when they are manifestly not;
- excessive mark-ups on so called green-products.

Nominations not falling into these categories were also welcomed.

Clearly this award, which is almost certain to attract considerable publicity, is concerned with the activities of business. But there could be a (negative) spin-off for any charities with a substantial sponsorship or promotional relationship with 'winning' companies.

The rather hastily organised 1989 Award required nominations by the first week of November 1989 – it may be that in future years this deadline will be brought forward. Winners were due to be announced at the end of 1989.

Future: There is a clear intention to repeat the award in future years.

Entry: On the official nomination form.

GREEN LEAF HOUSING AWARDS

New Homes Marketing Board, 82 New Cavendish Street, London W1M 8AD

Telephone: 071 580 5588

Contact: Gilly Greensitt, Communications Director
Sponsor: New Homes Marketing Board/House Builders Federation

This scheme, which is only open to housebuilders, is of relevance to charities because the awards (of £1000) are to be donated to the environmental charity of the recipient's choice. Interested charities should therefore monitor the local and national press to see if any local developments receive an award.

This scheme was launched in 1987. Entries fall into two categories. These are for housing on recycled, disused or derelict sites where the housebuilder has created a new landscape and one for housing on existing landscapes where the builder has blended the new building harmoniously with the established landscape. Any site in the UK completed three or more years ago is eligible. Those built more recently can be submitted for a provisional award until the landscape value can be properly assessed. Only housebuilders registered with the National House Building Council are eligible to enter. In 1989 six developments were given awards.

The deadline for entries in the 1990 competition was 31st January 1990, and the awards presentation was expected to be made in Spring 1990.

Future: We assume that the scheme will continue on an annual basis for the foreseeable future.

Entry: On the official entry form with photographic evidence.

GULBENKIAN MUSEUMS AND GALLERIES AWARDS

The Museums Association, 34 Bloomsbury Way, London, WC1A 2SF
Telephone: 071 404 4767

Contact: Mark Taylor/Caroline Lawton
Sponsor: Calouste Gulbenkian Foundation

This is a new competition, launched in 1989, to follow up Museums Year 1989. The awards are designed to recognise outstanding achievements and encourage improvements by Britain's public museums and galleries. They reward excellence, especially in education, resourcefulness, and the provision of good user-friendly facilities for visitors

A total of £5000 per year is available for prizes of which there will be eleven awards in all. They include:

£1000 for imaginative educational work;

£500 for the most improved museum or gallery in a rural area;

£500 for the best provision for disabled visitors, including blind people;

£250 for the best provision for young children;

£250 for the most improved catering facilities;

£500 for the most outstanding improvement achieved with limited resources.

The organisers state that 'credit will be given for friendly, well-informed and helpful staff, and for equal opportunities employers'.

There appear to be no restrictions on eligibility except that entries must relate to improvements and achievements undertaken in the previous year (since Januray 1989 in the case of the 1989/90 awards).

Entries for the 1989/90 competition had to be submitted by 31st December 1989. Winners were due to be announced in Spring 1990.

Future: The Calouste Gulbenkian Foundation and The Museums Association are committed to the scheme for at least the next three years.

Entry: On the official entry form with a short description (maximum

300 words) of the project – a separate statement is required in relation to each of the categories listed above. (We assume a single project may be entered in more than one category).

HABITAT AWARDS

Housing Foundation, Memorial Square, Coalville, Leicestershire LE6 4EU
Telephone: 0530 510444

Contact: Peter Elderfield (Director), Diane Deacon (Research Officer)

The Habitat Awards are designed to find and promote innovative human settlement projects in both developed and developing countries.

The awards were started as the Housing Foundation's contribution to the International Year of Shelter for the Homeless and, because of their success in attracting outstanding projects, have now become an annual event.

Two awards of £10,000 each are offered each year. Each award is divided into two – £2500 for the successful individual or organisation submitting the scheme and £7500 for a high quality presentation for the international promotion of the project.

Individuals, firms and other formally registered organisations are eligible to enter and entry is NOT restricted to UK residents. Where an existing project is submitted the submission must be made by either the original designers of the scheme or be accompanied by a letter from the designers permitting the scheme to be entered.

Previous entries may be resubmitted provided that the project has been further developed in the intervening period.

Schemes may be existing projects or projects designed specifically for the competition although preference will be given to the former.

They must be capable of being financially self-supporting or of attracting private or public funding, although preference will be given to those which do not rely upon substantial public funding. Evidence of provision of actual financial support would be welcome in submissions. Schemes should have the capacity of being applied in principle throughout most areas of the developed or developing world as appropriate. Schemes are sought which identify human settlement projects that offer sustainable futures to the residents and which present practical and imaginative solutions to current problems. All schemes should attempt to address associated problems of unemployment, diminishing energy reserves and a sustainable future as well as the direct housing problem. Suggested areas for consideration are as follows although entries need not be restricted to these:

Developed and developing countries
- Sustainable lifestyles in urban and/or rural areas.
- Energy efficient housing.
- Housing on a co-operative basis.
- Provision of shelter for the homeless.

Developed countries
- Inner city decay of housing and environment.
- Decline in towns and cities where main employment source has disappeared.

Developing countries
- Provision of low-cost housing for the poorest sector of the population.
- Slum dwellings and shanty towns of large urban areas.

Judging is a two stage process. Preliminary submissions (a typed summary of the project) should be sent before the end of July.

These are assessed and shortlisted entrants are then invited to submit more detailed proposals including plans, costings, and feasibility reports before the end of November.

Future: The organisers state that they intend to continue the Awards on an annual basis.

Entry: Initially typed submissions in English to the organisers. Full plans and diagrams are not required at this stage although a diagram showing the main features of the scheme would be appreciated. A detailed booklet on the award scheme is available from the organisers.

THE IAN ALLAN RAILWAY HERITAGE AWARDS

Awards address: The Association of Railway Preservation Societies, 6 Ullswater Grove, Alresford, Hants SO24 9NP

Contact: A. Harding
Sponsors: Ian Allan Ltd, British Rail, Railway Heritage Trust and British Coal.

ARPS administrative address: 3 Orchard Close, Watford, Hertfordshire, WD1 3DU (Telephone: 0923 221280)

The Ian Allan Railway Heritage Awards which have been run annually since 1979 are designed to 'applaud the best of railway building restoration and encourage the highest standards of care'. An attractive 10th Anniversary Brochure, published in 1989, states that 'Any railway building that has been, or is being restored can be entered – be it a great glass and iron extravagance, a magnificent gothic edifice, a wayside station in semi-domestic style or a humble piece of civil engineering. It does not matter who owns it; as part of our Railway Heritage, each building and structure deserves looking after.'

The competition has two categories of entry: volunteer projects which embrace most of Britain's 'preserved' railways and privately owned stations; and public and commercial projects covering all British Rail and London Underground stations and former railway structures now in alternative commercial or other use.

There are a variety of plaques and commendation certificates offered under each category. From 1989 a special award has been given for a specific aspect of the railway scene; in future years waiting rooms, signal boxes, footbridges, and static displays will come under special scrutiny. According to the literature available judges look for authentic, or visually sympathetic, restoration to a high standard of workmanship. 'Success does not depend upon major restoration ... simple cleaning, painting and refurbishment has won awards.... the emphasis is on quality of work, on sympathy of design and on the choice of materials, visual attractiveness and authenticity.' Replica and new structures are admissible entries.

Past winners have ranged from British Rail's extensive modernisation of Glasgow Central Station, to restoration of arguably Britain's smallest station (Damems) on the Keighley and Worth Valley Railway and the construction of a replica GWR terminus at Kidderminster.

Judges, drawn from a countrywide panel, inspect all entries in late summer and early autumn. Those gaining a high initial assessment receive a second visit from another judge. On the basis of these two independent assessments a panel of five national ajudicators makes the final selection in each category.

In 1989 the timetable for the Awards required entries to be submitted by 31st July 1989. Awards were due to be presented in March 1990 at a special ceremony at the Royal Society of Arts.

Future: There is every indication that this scheme will continue in future years.

Entry: On the official entry form with a £10 entry fee.

IDEAS ANNUAL COMPETITION

Action Match, c/o Community Links, Training and Development Unit, 14-18 West Bar Green, Sheffield, South Yorkshire S1 2DA

Telephone: 0742 723651

Contact: Mandy Wilson
Sponsor: Sponsorship being sought

Community Links publishes an Ideas Annual as a source of practical suggestions, good practice and inspiration in social and community action. As a means of encouraging people to submit ideas for inclusion in the Annual and of promoting the initiative, Action Match have launched a competition for the most inspiring and successful ideas in virtually any field of comunity activity. The organisers state that all ideas are welcome – 'they need not be grand or high-powered, it is often the smallest-scale ideas that touch people most'.

There are no restrictions on eligibility – the competition is genuinely open to anyone with a good idea. In 1989 there were three prizes: 'a laminated poster display on the work of your project, designed and made for and with you; a publicity leaflet written and produced with a professional advertising agency; and a choice of practical equipment (eg a loud-hailer, badge machine or creche toys)'.

The Ideas Annual '89 is structured according to the following headings which might be helpful to those submitting ideas: making people welcome, ways and means of working, getting messages across, taking services out into the community, participation and representation, exploiting local resources, co-operation, maintaining enthusiasm, consumer control, maximising potential, and pot pourri – which is anything else.

The 1989 competition required contributions/entries to be submitted by 15th August 1989.

Future: The organisers intend to repeat the competition, and the publication itself, annually.

Entry: No entry form – just submit contributions, maximum 500 words, to the organisers.

THE INDEPENDENT LIVING AWARDS

RADAR, 25 Mortimer Street, London W1N 8AB
Telephone: 071 637 5400

Contact: George Wilson, Director

There appears to be no published information about the scheme. The following is based on a summary written for us by George Wilson.

The Independent Living Awards, which were first given in 1989, are part of the European Community's HELIOS programme, the second four-year plan of action in favour of disabled people. The awards are designed to promote good practice in provision for disabled people. In 1989 awards were given in three categories:

- transport and mobility;
- access to public buildings;
- adapted housing and independent living.

An award can be made in each category in every (EC) member state. All award winners receive a prize of 2000 ECU.

Entry is by nomination rather than application. Nominations are made by the HELIOS national committee – in Britain this consists of members of government departments involved in various aspects of the HELIOS programme. Non-governmental organisations can also make nominations through their European associations. Judging of nominations is by a Community jury comprising one representative from each member state.

Future: RADAR expects the awards to be made again in 1990.

Entry: As outlined above the Awards are given on the basis of nominations. Organisations/projects which regard themselves as potential winners should ensure that RADAR and the relevant government departments are aware of their existence.

IT'S MY CITY

British Broadcasting Corporation, New Broadcasting House, PO Box 27 Oxford Road, Manchester M60 1SJ

Telephone: 061 200 2020

Contact: Clare Lewis

The first Its My City competition was launched in late 1988 and ran through to mid 1989. A second is planned for 1990. The following information is based on the material for 1988/89. Its My City is a 'nationwide contest to find Britain's most successful (urban) community projects'.

Individual schemes and projects involving urban and community regeneration based in towns or cities with a population of over 175,000 are eligible. Entries from towns, local authorities or 'large agencies' are NOT eligible. Schemes are judged on the following criteria: innovative, collaborative, growing, stimulating (generating hope and positive attitudes), locally focussed, participative (governed by and involving local people) and effective (able to demonstrate a clear outcome). In 1988/89 there were fourteen categories of project: advice/counselling, performing arts, visual arts, education/training, employment-general, environment/greening the city, equal opportunities, housing, leisure/recreation, social care, sports, tourism/heritage, and transport

The entry/judging procedure is as follows. Submitted entries, which are classified initially according to which city they represent, are assessed by panels of independent experts – the initial judging taking place regionally in London, Manchester and Glasgow. From this stage a shortlist of 12 cities, each represented by 10 projects, is prepared. The cities and projects are then visited by a judge or a member of the production team, and from these assessments six cities are chosen for filming – one film (programme) for each of the six cities featuring many of the projects and places entered in the competition. In 1989 the six cities were Belfast, Dundee, Leicester, Sunderland, Liverpool and Glasgow. Judges then select a shortlist of four projects ('finalists') from each category and from these the overall winner in each category is selected and featured in the 'final awards' programme. Note that shortlisted or winning projects need not be from the six cities featured in the television films.

Awards are cash prizes and considerable media exposure. (Some projects will be presented with their award on site, and this will be broadcast live as part of the final programme.)

Over 1000 entries were received for the 1988/89 competition. The organisers have also published a Project Directory containing over 700 entries – all projects entered into the competition. This is a most interesting publication in itself, as well as illustrating the very wide range of types of project which entered the competition.

For the 1988/89 competition entries had to be submitted by 31st December 1988 and the Its My City programmes were broadcast in late June 1989.

Future: We understand it is intended to run a competition in 1990, though we suspect the judging and assessment process might be streamlined a little.

Entry: On the official application form with one photograph (maximum 10'x8').

THE JAAP JOUSTRA AWARD FOR OUTSTANDING ACHIEVEMENT

Down's Syndrome Association, 12-13 Clapham Common Southside, London SW4 7AA

Telephone: 071 720 0008

Contact: Anna Khan
Sponsor: C & A Stores

This annual award, in memory of Jaap Joustra, a founder member of the Down's Syndrome Association, is presented to an adult with Down's Syndrome who has achieved something outstanding or has fulfilled their true potential in some aspect of their lives. Their achievement need not be spectacular nor a world first, but it should be one which has taken determination, application and perseverence on their part. Anyone over the age of 18 with Down's Syndrome may be nominated.

The prize for the overall winner is a special shield. In 1988 the winner and two runners-up received gift tokens and a camera and enjoyed a special lunch and presentation ceremony at the Cafe Royal in London. The overall winner in 1988 was Peter Wiseman for undertaking a sponsored parachute jump to raise funds for the Down's Syndrome Association – something which the Association recognised as 'requiring a lot of perseverence and determination for Peter to get accepted and a great deal of courage on the day of the jump'.

One of the runners-up was Lesley Black who 'applied herself with enthusiasm and determination' to her work as a trainee with Remploy and came second in the Grampian Region's Trainee of the Year competition. Of over 300 entrants she was the only one with any kind of handicap. Alan Saville was the other runner-up – his award in recognition of his transition from a large institution to a staffed group home and then to an independent life in his own flat.

Judging for the award is by an independent panel of celebrities and a DSA member with Down's Syndrome. The 1988 panel included a finalist from the previous year's competition – Ruth Polack. She commented '..this Award shows how to be independent when you have Down's Syndrome. We don't want to be treated like mentally handicapped mongols...'

The 1988 Award required nominations to be submitted by the end of January 1989.

Future: We assume the Award will continue for the forseeable future.

Entry: On the special nomination form which requires a statement (maximum of 500 words) on the reasons why the nominee deserves an award. There appear to be no restrictions on who may be a nominator although the permission of the nominee must be obtained prior to nomination.

THE JOHN HUNT AWARDS

The John Hunt Award Trust, c/o Intermediate Treatment Fund, 33 King Street, London WC2E 8JD

Telephone: 071 379 6171

Contact: Daphne Rawson-Jones, Correspondent

This scheme can be regarded as both a competition which recognises achievement and a small grant fund for existing and new projects. The Awards are for non-statutory, community-based enterprises in England and Wales which undertake activities to divert young people away from crime and into more constructive pursuits.

There are two main categories of award:

i) For projects involving groups of juvenile offenders who have made reparation to their communities; and

ii) For individual volunteers and voluntary groups (informal or registered) who have undertaken particularly noteworthy projects aimed at diverting juvenile offenders, and those at risk from criminal activities.

The judges, the trustees of The John Hunt Award Trust, will be looking for imaginative and effective use of local resources, community involvement and lasting benefit to young people and the community. The awards are up to £1000 in cash. They are given in recognition of achievements but must be used in furtherance of existing projects or to help fund new projects. How an award would assist the project or group entering is one of the criteria on which entries will be judged. Certificates of Merit may also be given to commercial organisations who have made significant efforts to help reduce juvenile crime in local communities.

In 1989 there were four awards of £1000 each and two of £500 each. A total of eight projects and individuals received Certificates of Merit. The major award winners were Piston Ring Youth Motorcycle Project in Warwickshire, Tong School Partnership in Bradford, Graigfelin Youth Activities Scheme in Swansea, and Youth Link Rhondda in Mid-Glamorgan.

Nominations may be submitted by leading members of the community in the voluntary and statutory sectors (eg Chair of local authority committees, Directors of Social Service, Chief Police Officers, Senior Youth Officers) and directly from projects themselves provided suitable references are given.

The closing date for entries in 1989 was 31st July. Awards were presented at a special ceremony in London in December. The organisers inform us that information for 1990 will be circulated in April 1990.

Future: We assume that the Awards will continue beyond 1990.

Entry: There are no entry forms. All is required is a letter describing the project or activity. This should cover its purpose, activities, membership (numbers of young people involved), the benefits achieved for the young people and the local community, and how an award would assist the work. The name and address of nominators, references where needed and a day-time telephone number should also be included.

THE JOHN MEJOR AWARD

Devon Conservation Forum, c/o County Hall, Exeter, Devon EX2 4QH
Telephone: 0392 273327

Contact: Ms Shan Toyne, Secretary
Sponsor: NALGO (Devon Branch) and Devon Conservation Forum

This annual award, which was initiated in 1986, aims to stimulate voluntary effort for environmental improvement throughout Devon and to provide recognition for the work done. To qualify entries must benefit Devon in at least one of the following ways:

a) to contribute to the visual or ecological improvement of the environment;

b) to help reduce the pressures on the county's wildlife, landscape and other natural resources;

c) to help towards integrating conservation principles with development policies in the context of the 1983 UK Conservation and Development programme.

Projects must have been completed within the two years prior to entry. Their scale is immaterial and the number of submissions per entrant is unlimited. Projects may be entered by all sectors of the community, including national and local environmental bodies, local authorities, companies, schools, youth groups and individuals. The only guideline for entrants is that they should 'demonstrate the environmental value of their submissions to enable judges to form a true assessment'. The organisers state that projects concerned solely with housing design should be entered into the separate Arnold Sayers Award which is also administered by the Devon Conservation Forum.

The awards take the form of certificates and cash prizes.

The 1988 winner was the Radford Adventure and Field Study Centre which is run by adults with learning difficulties. Second prize went to the Devon Birdwatching and Preservation Society for their 'Pocket Conservation Areas'. The presentation of the 1988 awards attracted considerable publicity for the winner and other prize winners on local radio and television and in the local press.

The deadline for entries to the 1989 competition was 30th September 1989.

Future: We assume the competition will continue.

Entry: There is no official entry form. Submissions should contain a letter of application , a brief description of the project, with at least two colour photographs and one in black and white (when appropriate) and a clear location plan.

LINCOLN CIVIC AWARD

The Trustees, Lincoln Civic Award, c/o Andrew and Co., St Swithin's Square, Lincoln LN2 1HB

Telephone: 0522 512123

Contact: Ms Jeanette Davies, Secretary to the Trustees

The purpose of this Award, which has been presented annually since 1966, is to 'express the thanks of the citizens of Lincoln to a person, or group of persons, to a society, to a company or to an organisation for an achievement which has...brought credit to the City and is itself of outstanding merit'. The organisers state that the award can be made in recognition of achievements in industry and commerce, or of an artistic, medical, social or religous nature or within the field of athletics or sport or leisure pursuits.

Examples given include: an employee in a local factory devising an invention of outstanding merit, a local artist who has a picture hung in the Royal Academy, a local athlete gaining a place in a national competition, or a group of local people undertaking work in the social field of outstanding value. The achievement may have been carried out as part of paid employment or voluntarily. The Award is a specially designed trophy, a solid silver obelisk, to be held for one year. A small silver medal or replica of the obelisk, to be retained by the winner, is also presented.

Nominations are invited by responsible organisations, industrialists employers or any individual and must be submitted by 31st March each year.

Future: The Awards and the Trust which administers the scheme were established by the Directors of Frank R Eccleshare Ltd as a perpetual mark of the Mayoralty of their colleague Frank R Eccleshare. The future of the Award seems assured.

Entry: Nominations on the official form or by letter should include full details of the person or group nominated, details of their achievements and names of referees.

LITERARY AWARDS

The Writers and Artists Yearbook (published by A & C Black, London) lists over 130 literary prizes and awards. The majority of these are only relevant to individual writers, poets, playwrights but there are some which we may of interest to those charities and voluntary organisations which publish their own books. Here are some examples:

Deloitte-Bookseller Award for the best cover design for any book in any category. Open to all UK based designers and design teams – £1000.
Contact: Victoria Pugh, The Media Group, Deloitte Haskins and Sells, Po Box 207, 128 Queen Victoria Street, London, EC4P 4JX. tel 071 248 3913

The Fawcett Book Prize for the book which does the most to illuminate women's position in society today – £500.
Contact: General Secretary, The Fawcett Society, 46 Harleyford Road, London, SE11 5AY

Sir Peter Kent Conservation Book Prize for the best book on environmental issues published in the UK – £1500.
Contact: Book Trust, Book House, 45 East Hill, London

MIND Book of the Year – the Allen Lane Award for a book which 'outstandingly furthers public understanding of the prevention, causes, treatment or experience of mental illness or mental handicap' – £1000.
Contact: Christine Shaw, MIND, 22 Harley Street, London W1N 2ED

Odd Fellows (Manchester Unity) Social Concern Annual Book Awards for a book or pamphlet in an area of social concern – £2000.
Contact: Book Trust, Book House, 45 East Hill, London SW18 2QZ

LIVEWIRE

Livewire UK, 60 Grainger Street, Newcastle upon Tyne NE1 5JG
Telephone: 091 261 5584

Contact: Peter Westgarth, UK Director
Sponsor: Shell UK Ltd

Livewire is a national programme to encourage and support youth enterprise. It embraces a number of initiatives designed to both help individual young entrepreneurs and develop a network of supporting projects and services around the country. Livewire coordinates a network of local advisers, publishes a range of materials and organises training events to help young people setting up and running small businesses. Livewire runs two competitions – the Start-Up Awards and the In-Business Challenge.

The Start-Up Awards Competition is open to any 16 to 25 year old whose business was not trading before July 1989 (in the case of the 1989/90 Awards). Entrants are initially judged on their submitted Business Plan. Entrants are judged at county level and then each county nominates one entrant to go forward to one of the ten National or English Regional rounds. The winner in each of these rounds receives a £1000 prize and is forwarded to the United Kingdom final. Other awards of cash and in-kind help are made at regional level. The overall UK winner – 'the most promising new young business' – receives an additional £3000 prize. The timetable, in 1990, for the Start-Up Awards required initial entries to be submitted by 28th February 1990. The final was scheduled for mid May 1990 with the overall UK winner announced on May 22nd.

The In-Business Challenge was launched in May 1990. Entry is by nomination from agencies, individuals or by Livewire invitation, and is open to 16 to 30 year olds whose business is trading. The structure of the competition is similar to that for the Start-Up Awards in that nominations are judged locally and then forwarded to National and English Regional rounds, each with a top prize of £1000. Regional winners are entered for the UK In-Business Challenge. The In-Business Challenge takes the form of an outdoor management training weekend linked to individual business development plans.

Future: We assume that the recently restructured Livewire programme, including the competitions, will continue for the foreseeable future.

Entry: Entry to the Start-Up Awards is by completed entry form to be submitted with a Business Plan. Entry forms are included in the

Action Pack sent to those who request advice and support from Livewire and are also available from local Livewire Coordinators, enterprise agencies and youth enterprise centres. Entry to the In-Business Challenge is by nomination – contact Livewire Head Office or local Coordinators for details. Nominees are required to complete a business development questionnaire which must returned with supporting information.

MAYOR OF BOURNEMOUTH VOLUNTEER OF THE YEAR AWARD

Mayor's Parlour, Town Hall, Bournemouth BH2 6DY
Telephone: 0202 292366

Contact: Ms Diana Sands, Mayor's Secretary

This award, to coincide with Volunteers Week, is designed to recognise and reward volunteers who support others in any walk of life. The award 'covers the Borough of Bournemouth' which we assume means that the voluntary work involved must benefit individuals or the wider community of the Borough, rather than requiring entrants to reside or be based in the Borough.

Two awards are offered: for individuals and for groups. The organisers offer the following guidelines on the types of activity which would be eligible:

- voluntary work involving help for those disadvantaged by age, handicap, sickness or lack of knowledge or experience;

- work of benefit to the environment by contributing to the improvement of a community or its facilities;

- the involvement of young people directly or indirectly with services to themselves or others;

- personal sacrifice of an individual or group to support less fortunate members of the community;

- raising money for worthwhile projects.

Both awards take the form of a cup, to be held for one year, and a Commendation Certificate. Judging is by a panel of leading personalities. For the 1989 Awards entries had to be submitted by 4th October with the award presented on 1st November 1989. There appear to be no restrictions on who may make nominations.

Future: The continuation of these Awards depends entirely on the Mayor in office at the time.

Entry: Nominations on the official form.

MERSEY BASIN CAMPAIGN AWARDS

Mersey Basin Campaign Voluntary Sector Network, 111 The Piazza, Piccadilly Plaza, Manchester M1 4AN

Telephone: 061 228 6924

Contact: Phil Barton/Erica Jones
Sponsor: Unilever

This is a new award scheme which in its first year in 1989 focussed on 'Waterside Revival'.

The 1989 Waterside Revival Awards were open to all voluntary organisations, community groups, schools and individuals who had completed a waterside project, large or small, or a significant part of a project within the two years prior to the closing date for entries – 13th October 1989. To be eligible the project must be located in the Mersey Basin or Leeds and Liverpool canal corridor, and thus in one of the following local authority districts:

Lancashire: West Lancashire, Chorley, Blackburn, Hyndburn, Burnley, Pendle, Rossendale.

Merseyside: Sefton, Liverpool, Knowsly, St Helens, Wirral.

Derbyshire: High Peak.

Cheshire: Ellesmere Port and Neston, Chester, Vale Royal, Macclesfield, Halton, Warrington, Congleton, Crewe and Nantwich.

Greater Manchester: Wigan, Bolton, Bury, Rochdale, Oldham, Salford, Manchester, Tameside, Trafford, Stockport.

The judges were looking for sustained effort by local people in improving the waterside for the benefit of their community and finding new uses for neglected assets – whether buildings, landscape or a stretch of water. The judging team included representatives of Manchester Council for Voluntary Service and Granada Reports, the Acting Conservator of the River Mersey, Sir John Tavare, Chairman of the Mersey Basin Campaign, and Mike Harding, entertainer and patron of the Mersey Basin Voluntary Sector Network.

Entries had to be submitted by 13th October 1989 with winning entrants presented with their prizes later that same month. Granada Television was committed to covering the launch of the scheme and featuring winners in their Granada Reports programme. Prizes took the form of trophies and cash awards of £500 for first, £200 for second and £100 for third prize. In addition awards of £100 were made to the best school project and the best project by an individual.

Future: At the time of writing, the 1989 competition had only just been completed and we are uncertain as to its continuation in current or adapted form.

Entry: On the official entry form.

MIDLANDS WOMEN OF THE YEAR AWARDS

Midlands Women of the Year, Hall Cottage, Holme Pierrepoint, Nottingham NG12 2LD

Contact: June Lawrie, Secretary
(See below for address for submission of nominations)
Sponsor: Elizabeth Arden

This is an interesting award scheme, in that as well as giving public recognition for personal achievement, it has also proved to be a very effective fundraising vehicle. These awards, founded in 1983 by the current Secretary, are designed to honour 'exceptional' women in the following three categories:

Business: a woman who has displayed exceptional business skills – who has made a significant contribution to the financial performance of her company and may even have set up her own firm – proving herself to be a true entrepreneur.

Achievement: a woman who has reached a high point in her life without any thought of personal gain – she may have excelled in sport or the arts, or contributed outstanding service in the field of voluntary work.

Courage: a woman who has shown outstanding courage by risking her life to help others or who has battled against the odds whilst fighting a disability to achieve a normal family life or hold down a demanding job.

Nominations may be submitted by anyone – for the 1990 Awards the deadline is the second week in August. Judging of the eighteen finalists (six in each category) who have come through the regional finals takes place in September. The awards are presented at a special luncheon in October. The luncheon, which in 1989 was attended by 650 women, is a regular major fundraising event generating about £14,000 each year for the Winged Fellowship's Midlands Holiday Centre at Holme Pierrepoint. Individuals and companies are invited to 'sponsor' an invitation to the luncheon, or a whole table, for people, perhaps employees or colleagues, who they wish to acknowledge and recognise for their own achievements.

Future: The Awards are well established and are likely to continue.

Entry: Official nomination forms are available from:

Carol Pochiol: Manthorpe Engineering Ltd, Manthorpe House, Brittain Drive, Codnor Gate Industrial Estate, Ripley, Derbyshire, DE5 3QB, Telephone: 0773 43555

Sandra Squires: Chart Foulkes Lynch plc, 82 New Street, Birmingham, B2 4BA, Telephone: 021 633 3543

MUSEUM OF THE YEAR AWARDS

National Heritage, 9a North Street, London SW4 0HN
Telephone: 071 720 6789

Contact: Pauline Lawson-Smith
Sponsor: British Gas plus other subsidiary sponsors (see below)

(Note that National Heritage is an independent organisation, and registered charity which styles itself 'The Museums Action Movement'. It is unrelated to the government agency, English Heritage.)

These awards were first made in 1973, and have been made continuously ever since. Although the term 'museum' is used throughout the promotional literature for the awards and in this entry, the scheme does embrace 'museums, art galleries and similar institutions'. The awards are open to all museums in the United Kingdom in membership of National Heritage. (Application for membership can coincide with the submission of an entry for the award.)

The overall aims and purpose of this award scheme are to encourage and reward new initiatives in museums 'beyond the call of duty'. The overall winner is that museum which is judged most 'outstanding'. The intention of the organisers is to choose a museum as a winner whose example the judges have a reasonable hope will influence other museums for the better. The awards may be offered for either new museums or established museums which have effected one or more notable new projects or special exhibitions, although in all cases museums will be judged as 'totalities – not solely in respect of particular items'.

There are normally six main awards offered each year although these may vary according to the support of subsidiary sponsors. The 1990 Awards were as follows:

National Heritage Museum of the Year – the most outstanding overall. A specially commissioned trophy by Dame Elisabeth Frink and £2000 (sponsored by British Gas)

Best museum of industrial or social history: £1500 (sponsored by Unilever Ltd)

Best entry in fine art or applied art section: £1500 (sponsored by Phillips Fine Art Auctioneers and Valuers)

Best museum of archaeological or historical interest: £1000 (sponsored by BBC History and Archaeology Unit)

Best educational programme in a museum: £1000 (sponsored by BP)

Entrant 'achieving the most with the least': Costume figure (sponsored by Museum Casts Ltd)

The organisers state that judges will bear in mind 'the great difference in status, size and resources of individual museums and will take these factors into consideration in making the awards'.

Entries are assessed by a panel of judges, which in 1989/90 was chaired by Sir Hugh Casson – a Council Member of National Heritage.

All entries are visited by at least one judge and in many cases by three or four.

The timetable for the 1990 awards required entries to be submitted by 30th June 1989. Entries should relate to museums opened or improvements/projects/exhibitions instituted during the previous year (1st July 1988 to 1st July 1989). Winners are announced in the Museums Bulletin of The Museums Association and in the Judges Report published by National Heritage and circulated to its members. British Gas publicised the overall 1989 winner (The National Portrait Gallery at Bodelwyddan Castle Museum) and their sponsorship of the award in the national press.

Future: We assume this scheme will continue although specific categories of award may vary according to the availability of sponsorship.

Entry: On the official form together with supporting material including photographs, brochures, press cuttings, etc in an A4 folder. Three unmounted black and white photographs (preferably 9'x7') should be submitted. If the entrant is not already a member of National Heritage, a fee of £20 which automatically gives membership for one year should also be sent.

MUSEUMS YEAR AWARD

This award scheme was launched in 1989 to mark Museums Year. It was organised by the Museums Association and sponsored by Shell UK Ltd and The Times. However, we understand that although the scheme may continue after 1989, the Museums Association will no longer be associated with it in any way.

The scheme is designed to 'reward museums and galleries which have demonstrated the most innovative approach to public programming during the year'. There were two major awards offered in 1989/90. These were The Museums Year Award for £20,000 and the Community Museum of the Year Award for £10,000. The latter award recognises museums or galleries whose work has aided the development of their locality and who have forged a solid and interactive relationship with the local community. A further award was offered to the museum professional who has contributed significantly to the success of his/her museum or gallery.

The organisers define a museum or gallery as an institution with a collection as well as an exhibition space. 'The awards are not open to tourist attractions that are not strictly museums or art galleries.' The entry procedure is based on nominations (in the two main categories) submitted by readers of The Times. A panel of expert judges reviews these nominations and prepares a shortlist of five in each category. These are then voted upon by Times readers to decide the overall winners. The panel of judges also determines the winner of the individual museum professional award.

The scheme was officially launched on 19th June 1989, and winners were announced at a ceremony in December.

Future: Uncertain

Entry: Nominations via readers of The Times although this arrangement could change in future years, if the scheme continues.

NFCO PUBLICITY COMPETITION

National Federation of Community Organisations, 8/9 Upper Street London N1 0PQ

Telephone: 071 226 0189

Contact: Katy Lofters
Sponsor: Gifts for Giving Ltd (in 1989)

A competition exclusively for community associations and similar bodies in membership of the National Federation of Community Organisations. The competition is for effective publicity activities/material in the following three categories:

a) A poster publicising an event run by the entrant;

b) A Community Newsletter or Magazine published by the entrant (one issue to be submitted);

c) A Community Centre Noticeboard (a photograph to be submitted).

Entries, which are judged by representatives of NFCO and the sponsors, are assessed on: their effectiveness in achieving their purpose, their cost-effectiveness and their accessibility to all members of the community. Prizes in 1989 were an electronic typewriter for first, and an information board with detachable letters for second, in each of the three categories listed above.

The deadline for entries in 1989 was 4th August. Prizes were presented and the winning entries displayed at the NFCO Annual Conference.

Future: 1989 was the first year of this competition. Its continuation with the same or a different focus in 1990 has not yet been confirmed. All NFCO members will automatically receive details.

Entry: There is no entry form. As well as the relevant material (copies of poster or magazine/newsletter, or photographs of noticeboard) entrants are asked to submit a note saying 'who you were aiming at, what was your purpose, what costs were involved and what were the results.'

THE NORFOLK SOCIETY AWARDS

The Norfolk Society, c/o Fielden and Mawson, Ferry Road, Norwich NR1 1SU

Contact: Geoffrey Mitchell, Chairman of Awards Committee (Note that this is the name and address of the Awards' organiser and not the address of the Secretary of The Norfolk Society which is 19, Chenery Drive, Sprowston, Norwich, NR7 8RR.)

Sponsor: Eastern Counties Newspapers

Each year this scheme offers a number of awards in recognition of the achievements of individuals and organisations in helping to preserve or enhance the attraction of the environment of Norfolk. The awards are generally for projects in the rural parts of the county. (The Norfolk Society also acts as the Norfolk branch of the Council for the Protection of Rural England.) The Chairman of the Awards Committee commented at the presentation of the 1987/88 awards that the scheme was to 'say thank you to those people who have put in the energy and the vision to produce good work' and 'to blow the trumpet for them so that others can follow their example'.

Any scale of project is eligible although the organisers are especially keen to recognise smaller ones – 'it is the sum total of individual efforts, large and small, which maintains the attraction of the countryside, and no achievement is rated too small to be considered'.

Winners in 1987/88 included: the recording of the flora and fauna of Wheatfen Broad by the late Ted Ellis; the conversion (into a workshop) of a tythe barn; the re-creation of a 1912 worker's cottage garden at the Gressenhall Rural Life Museum; and the creation of a new broad (the first this century) at How Hill. There were seven awards in all – winners received a plaque and certificates were presented by BBC Radio presenter John Timpson.

Entries for the 1988/89 awards had to be submitted by 14th November 1988. Winners were presented with their awards at the Society's AGM in March.

Future: This scheme appears to be a popular and well supported activity of the Norfolk Society and seems likely to continue.

Entry: On the official application form. At least two black and white photographs (likely to be the basis for initial judging) should be included. Entries may come from any source – it is acceptable for projects/activities to be 'nominated' although the permission of the owner or key individual(s) involved must be obtained first.

NORTH YORK MOORS NATIONAL PARK CONSERVATION AWARDS

North York Moors National Park Department, the Old Vicarage, Bondgate, Helmsley, North Yorkshire YO6 5BP

Telephone: 0439 70657

Contact: DC Statham, National Park Officer
Sponsor: Robert Thompson – the 'Mouseman of Kilburn'

This annual scheme, first run in 1989/90, recognises and encourages action by schools to conserve the natural environment of the National Park. 'Any project [by a school] which makes a tangible and exemplary contribution to the conservation of the area's natural beauty will qualify. This will encompass projects which conserve or enhance the natural history of the National Park, as well as projects which preserve or enhance its visual attractiveness.' Any conservation project within the National Park will be eligible although all schools within the counties of North Yorkshire and Cleveland may enter. Projects must be complete, or substantially so, at the time of entry.

There are two separate classes: for junior/middle schools and for secondary schools. Winning projects in each class receive a wooden plaque to keep for one year, a permanent memento and a cash prize to enable the school to buy tools and embark on a further project. The judges are the Chairman and Vice-Chairman of the National Park Committee who will look for evidence of thorough preparation and planning as well as a sensitive approach to implementation.

Entries should be submitted by 31st March 1990 and judging is due to take place shortly afterwards.

Future: This scheme is intended to be run annually.

Entry: On the official entry form with appropriate supporting material. The organisers are pleased to offer advice to potential entrants.

NORTHUMBERLAND TREE AND HEDGEROW CUP COMPETITION

Northumberland County Council, Department of Planning and Economic Development, County Hall, Morpeth, Northumberland, NE61 2EF

Telephone: 0670 514343

Contact: Geoffrey Creighton, Principal Landscape Architect
Sponsors: Tweeddale Press Group/Journal newspaper/ Northumberland Wildlife Trust

The aim of this competition is to focus attention on the environmental importance of well maintained trees and hedgerows and give recognition to those who are playing their part in maintaining the attractive landscape of Northumberland. The competition was launched in 1978 and has become an annual event. Entry is open to any individual or organisation although in most years the majority of entries are from farmers and private landowners. The entered scheme must be located in Northumberland.

The focus of the competition varies from year to year. In 1989 there were two categories of entry as follows:

• Broadleaved woodlands – for a single woodland or a group of separate areas not exceeding four hectares and not more than 25 years old in rural or urban landscapes.

• New Hedgerows – planted in the last five years and not necessarily in an agricultural landscape.

The winner in each category receives a cup and the first three receive certificates and cash prizes totalling £100. There are two further special awards which are regularly part of the competition – for the submission which contributes most to wildlife conservation (offered by Northumberland Wildlife Trust) and for the best notional tree planting scheme planned by a Young Farmers' Club.

Future: A well established scheme which we assume will continue.

Entry: A simple entry form is included on publicity material and this must be completed and returned. Brief details of the type and location of the entry (with a location map) are required.

PRIDE OF PLACE AWARDS

The David Knightly Charitable Trust, 22 Queensdale Road, Holland Park, London W11 4QB

Contact: Chair

The Pride of Place Awards provide grants for practical schemes aimed at improving the environment and raising the level of awareness amongst the public to environmental issues.

The scheme, organised and funded by The David Knightly Trust, is not for projects completed or in progress, but is designed as a pump-primer to give voluntary organisations an incentive to raise the balance of funds they require. Trustees are particularly anxious to assist practical environmental improvement schemes in villages, towns and cities which will be of maximum benefit to the community. Sympathetic consideration will be given to imaginative schemes which might serve as models for the solution of similar problems elsewhere. Projects must be completed within eighteen months of an award being offered. We have no information on the geographical eligibility for the scheme.

Applications must be submitted by the end of February in order to be assessed by trustees at their spring meeting. There would appear to be no formal presentation ceremonies or other publicity – indeed the tone of the scheme is rather low key.

Future: We assume the Trust will continue to run this scheme.

Entry: There is no application form. Applications should include plans and photographs illustrating the site and proposed work, costings, a financial statement revealing how much money has been raised and how the rest might be obtained. Applicants must show that the necessary consents have been obtained. 'Brevity and conciseness should be the aim for the mutual benefit of applicants and Trustees alike.'

THE PRINCE OF WALES' AWARD

The Prince of Wales' Committee, 4th Floor, Empire House, Mount Stuart Square, Cardiff
Telephone: 0222 471121

Contact: Award Group Secretary
Sponsor: The Midland Bank

This scheme was established in 1970 to recognise individuals and organisations who have undertaken outstanding projects to improve the Welsh environment or promote understanding of the environment.

Any individual, group or organisation, including any commercial or statutory body, is eligible to enter. Projects entered must have been completed within the eighteen months preceding the closing date of entry. Judges look for projects which are innovative or develop existing concepts and which are carefully designed and executed. They take into account the level of resources available to the entrants. Entries from schools and youth organisations are encouraged and may be for study projects as well as for practical work. Examples of previous winners illustrate the breadth of the scheme: an international company for the design and landscaping of a new factory, a farmer for an educational trail, a local authority for renovating an historic industrial village, primary school children for creating a local museum and a scout troop for helping to preserve an historic chapel.

Awards take the form of certificates which are presented by HRH The Prince of Wales at a special ceremony. Entries from business and commerce are automatically entered for a special award given by the Institute of Directors in Wales. There is no limit to the number of awards which may be made – entries are judged on their own merits and not in competition with each other.

The Awards are just part of the Committee's activities aimed at encouraging and developing environmental improvements in urban and rural Wales. The Committee also provides advice, support and in some cases grant aid, acts as a forum for discussion of 'the forces influencing the environment' and promotes environmental education.

The deadline for entries is 15th June each year. Awards are normally presented in late November or early December of the same year.

Future: A well established scheme which we assume will continue.

Entry: On the official entry form with four colour slides and relevant plans, maps and other photographs.

PRUDENTIAL AWARDS FOR THE ARTS

Kallaway Limited, 2 Portland Road, Holland Park, London, W11 4LA
Telephone: 071 221 7883

Contact: Administrator, Prudential Awards for the Arts
Sponsor: Prudential Corporation

Publicised as 'the country's richest ever annual Arts Awards' offering a total of £200,000 in prizes. The scheme is administered by the arts management company Kallaway Ltd on behalf of Prudential Corporation and is 'presented in association with' the Arts Council of Great Britain. The Awards are 'open to organisations throughout the UK in the performing and visual arts, no matter their size or status'. 'The criteria for judging the Awards is based upon consistent innovation and creativity, coupled with excellence and accessibility in the arts, with the aim of widening the audience and establishing greater understanding and enjoyment of the discipline.'

The scheme has five categories – the winner in each receives £25,000.

The categories are: dance (classical ballet to contemporary dance); music (jazz bands to symphony orchestras); opera (grand opera to music theatre); theatre (established to fringe); and visual arts (galleries to open-air parks). The overall winner, chosen from the category winners, receives an additional £75,000. The Arts Council also makes a special Award to the person who 'has made an outstanding individual contribution to the furtherance of innovation and creativity in the Arts'.

Entry is open to 'professional arts organisations and amateur organisations provided they are professionally managed and based in the UK. Entrants must have been practising, promoting or presenting the performing and/or visual arts, not for profit, for at least two years before 1st November 1988 [in the case of the 1989 Awards]'.

The detailed 'Rules and Conditions' state that 'awards money shall be spent by the winning organisations in the development of their artistic programme. It shall not be spent on the repayment of deficits, capital improvements or capital costs in general'. All Award winners must include the Award logo on promotional material associated with their planned programme.

The winners of the 1989 Awards were The Almeida Theatre (Music Award), Common Ground (Visual Arts), Communicado (Theatre), English National Opera (Opera), and Rambert Dance Company (Dance and overall winner). The win for Common Ground in particular should encourage entries from smaller organisations whose work involves 'the arts' in a broad and imaginative way.

The closing date for entries was 31st January 1988, with first stage judging between November 1988 and July 1989 and second stage judging between July 1989 and October 1989. The Awards presentation took place on 29th October 1989.

Future: The organisers state that the Awards will run for a minimum of three years.

Entry: On the official Entry Form. Further printed supporting material may be submitted at the time of entry.

RATCLIFF MOBILITY AWARD

Ratcliff Tail Lifts Ltd, Bessemer Road, Welwyn Garden City, Herts
Telephone: 0707 325571

Contact: Cambell McKee
Sponsor: Ratcliff Tail Lifts Ltd

This scheme is for individuals, groups or organisations, who have made the greatest contribution to improving travel for people with mobility problems. The organisers give illustrations of some of the types of schemes which would be eligible. These include:

- a new or improved item of equipment which assists the mobility of disabled people;
- a new or improved service for people with a mobility handicap;
- a major commitment to increasing public awareness of the mobility needs of disabled people.

Three awards are offered: £1000, a silver medal and certificate for first and £500 and a certificate for each of two runners-up.

Judging is carried out by representatives of the organisers, the Department of Transport and RADAR. A recent winner of an award is Tripscope – a new national information and advice service for disabled and elderly travellers.

In 1989 the closing date for entries was 31st March, and the awards were presented during the Mobility Roadshow at the Transport and Road Research Laboratory at Crowthorne in mid-June 1989.

Future: We understand from the organisers that they do plan to run the scheme again in 1990.

Entry: On the official nomination form. Entries may be nominated by 'third parties' – ie individuals or organisations not directly connected with the 'projects' concerned. Names and addresses of two independent referees are required. A single nominator may make no more than three nominations.

REFORM 'COMPASSIONATE ACTION' TRUST AWARD

Charities Aid Foundation, 48 Pembury Road, Tonbridge, Kent TN9 2JD
Telephone: 0732 771333

Contact: Promotions Department, Reform (EG) Charitable Trust, 21 John Adam Street, London WC2N 6JG
Telephone: 071 930 8965

Contact: Douglas Llambias, Chairman of Trustees

(Further information on the scheme should be obtained from CAF, but entries submitted to The Reform Charitable Trust.)

The scheme is part of The Reform Club's long standing work 'to encourage social and charitable progress'. It is designed to recognise the outstanding contribution made to UK and overseas charities by those working both in the 'public eye' and 'behind the scenes'. In 1989 there were two categories of awards. One for the individual judged to have made the most exceptional achievement on behalf of their chosen charity by: demonstrating unique leadership skills, raising awareness, raising funds, or showing commitment and plain hard work. The second award was made to a member of the public in recognition of their outstanding contribution to charity in one or more of the following ways: raising funds, enthusiastic commitment, dedication to the cause, and outstanding service.

Nominations may be made by charities and voluntary organisations. A single nominator may nominate one candidate for each award.

The winner in each category receives a cash prize of £1000 and a personal replica of the award trophy. The closing date for entries was 30th July 1989 and awards were presented at The Reform Club in late 1989/early 1990.

Future: We assume the scheme will continue in some form.

Entry: Nominations must be in the form of a citation of no more than 150 words. They must be submitted to The Reform Club – address as above.

RICS CONSERVATION AWARDS

The Royal Institution of Chartered Surveyors, 12 Great George Street, Parliament Square, London SW1P 3AD

Telephone: 071 222 7000

Contact: Suzy Reich, Press and Publicty Officer

Up to the end of 1988 The Royal Institution of Chartered Surveyors (RICS) in conjunction with The Times had for many years run a national Conservation Awards Scheme. In 1988 this focussed on projects involving the provision or improvement of public facilities 'for the enjoyment of the countryside and rural coastline while at the same time conserving or enhancing the landscape.'

This particular scheme has been discontinued, but we understand that RICS will be launching a new 'set of award schemes' in March 1990.

Categories in these new awards will include 'conservation and urban renewal as well as other issues relevant to chartered surveyors'.

Future: No further information is available at the time of writing. In the past, awards have been open to both privately and publicly funded projects and entries accepted from public authorities, companies, professional practices and private individuals.

Entry: We suggest you register your interest with RICS at the above address.

THE RIGHT LIVELIHOOD AWARDS

Research Office, School of Peace Studies, University of Bradford, Bradford, West Yorkshire BD7 1DP
Telephone: 0274 737143
(Administrative office for the Awards until March 1990)

42, Warriner Gardens, London SW11 4DU
(Home address for Paul Ekins, Research Director of the Foundation)

(The Right Livelihood Awards Foundation, which organises these awards, is due to move its office base to Sweden in March 1990. We suggest that you contact either of the above to obtain their current address.)

These Awards were introduced in 1980 'to honour and support those working on practicable and replicable solutions to the real problems facing us today'. They recognise 'vision and work contributing to making life more whole, healing our planet and uplifting humanity.' The idea came from Jakob von Uexkull, a Swedish-German writer and philatelist, who sold his valuable stamp collection to provide the initial endowment which has funded the awards. Von Uexkull, who remains Chairman of the Foundation, felt that the Nobel prizes had become too narrow and specialised in focus and ignored much work and knowledge vital for the survival of mankind. It is no surprise that the media tend to refer to the awards as 'the Alternative Nobel Prizes'.

Nominations may be made by anyone in the world for both individuals and organisations. In the case of the latter, nominations may not be made by employees or key workers. Self-nomination is not acceptable. Awards take two forms – cash, totalling at least US$100,000 to be shared by several recipients and a non-monetary award presented to a person whose work the (international) jury wishes to honour and recognise but who is not primarily in need of monetary support. The cash award is to be used for specific projects and not for personal use.

Since 1980, 40 people have been chosen for awards from 250 nominations from 50 different countries. In recent years four or five awards have been given each year. Recipients in 1988 were Dr Inge Kemp Genefke of the International Rehabilitation and Research Centre for Torture Victims, Jose Lutzenberger for environmental conservation work in Brazil, John Turner for championing the rights of people to build and manage their own communities, and the Sahabat Alam (Friends of the Earth) movement in Malaysia.

The timetable for the Awards requires nominations to be submitted by 31st May each year. Presentations are made on the day before the announcement of the Nobel Prizes in December.

Future: We assume these Awards will continue – they are the only function of The Right Livelihood Awards Foundation

Entry: There is no official 'entry form' although the organisers offer guidelines for nominators and nominees. A short history of the project concerned, biographies of the founders/leaders/members, written material about the project or produced by it, length of project, number of paid and unpaid staff, and annual budget. Nominators are also asked to stipulate whether the nomination is for a cash or honorary award and whether the nominee can respond to the requests for information which would follow an award and is prepared to share information with others.

ROYAL INSURANCE YOUNG CRITIC AWARD

c/o Kallaway Ltd, 2 Portland Road, London W11 4LA
Telephone: 071 221 7883

Contact: Elizabeth Dudley/Claire Robinson
Sponsor: Royal Insurance

This scheme, first launched in September 1989, offers awards for the best critical reviews of any live performance or television programme by 14 to 16 year olds. One of the judges regards the scheme as 'excellent because it encourages pupils to consider the important role the critic plays in analysing what goes into making a performance good, or bad'. The scheme is seen as an extension of Royal Insurance's sponsorship of the Royal Shakespeare Company.

Judges are looking for reviews which 'stand up to scrutiny, are incisive, entertaining or thought provoking'. The Award is for individual entries although a maximum of only four entries per school may be submitted. Entries should be between 500 and 600 words long.

The organisers state that 'teachers may wish to run a class project as the review is eligible as part of the GCSE Drama/English course work requirements for the Mode 1 exam'.

The overall winner receives £125, £2000 for his/her school to spend on educational visits and a trip to the RSC for up to 50 classmates for a perfomance of his/her own choice. Second and third prize winners will receive respectively £75 and £25 and a visit to the RSC.

Judges in 1989 included Michael Billington of The Guardian, writer Susan Hill, and artistic director of the National Youth Theatre Edward Wilson.

The 1989 scheme was launched in September 1989 with a closing date for entries of 31st January 1990.

Future: The organisers state that 'if the level and quality of submissions is high, it is expected to run [the scheme] annually'.

Entry: One official entry form per school which should include the names and addresses of up to four individual entrants. This should be submitted with the clearly handwritten or typed reviews. Candidates wishing to submit their entry for GCSE examination should send only photocopies as manuscripts will not be returned.

ROYAL MAIL SPORTS CLUB AWARD SCHEME

Telephone and contact: see text

Sponsor: Royal Mail Letters

This scheme aims to assist sports clubs to develop by matching every £1 raised with an additional £2 for agreed projects, schemes or new equipment up to a value of £3,000. All award winners are entered into a Club of the Year Competition with an additional prize of £3000.

The scheme is run in association with the Sports Council (in England), the Northern Ireland Sports Council, the Sports Council for Wales, and the Scottish Sports Council.

In England, the following sports are eligible for support under this scheme: athletics, tennis, basketball, football, fencing, gymnastics, volleyball, field hockey, swimming, diving and water polo.

Elsewhere, any sport recognised by the national Sports Council for grant aid is eligible. In Wales the emphasis has been on projects which encourage youth participation in sport (such as links between schools and clubs, come and try days, promotion days, schemes to support young sporting talent, activities to promote membership, School of Sport/ coaches/ courses/ events.

Entry: Applications are considered throughout the year. Application forms are available from sports governing bodies, local Sports Council officers or the contacts below:

England
Alan Pascoe Associates, 141-143 Drury Lane, London WC2B 5TB. Tel. 071-379 5220. Contact: Jane Allbury.

Northern Ireland
Northern Ireland Sports Council, Upper Malone Road, Belfast BT9 5LA. Tel. 0232-381222. Contact: Danny O'Connor.

Wales
Sports Council for Wales, Sophia Gardens, Cardiff CF1 9SW. Tel. 0222-397571. Contact: John Stevens.

Scotland
Scottish Sports Council, St Colme Street, Edinburgh EH3 6AA. Tel. 031-225 8411. Contact: Aileen Simpson.

ROYAL MAIL YOUNG LETTER-WRITERS COMPETITION

for more information: Royal Mail Headquarters, Room 195, 33 Grosvenor Place, London SW1X 1PX

for submission of entries: Secrets Competition, Freepost, Northampton NN3 1BR. ('Secrets' was the theme of the 1989 Competition.)

The competition is clearly designed to encourage letter-writing by young people – an activity in which the organisers and sponsors have an obvious commercial interest. The competition appears to be an annual event – with a different theme each year. Judges look for 'interesting and exciting letters, full of your own thoughts and ideas' in addition to legibility, correctly presented addresses and so on. The competition is open to young people under the age of 17 (on 31st August 1989 for the 1989 scheme) and resident in the UK. Entries are judged in three age groups as follows:

Group A: Under 9 years on 31st August 1989;

Group B: 9 to 13 years on 31st August 1989;

Group C: 13 to under 17 years on 31st August 1989.

The prizes are substantial for both the individual and his/her school. In 1989 the winners in each age group received the following:

First: £400 and a 'secret' prize, and an Archimedes Computer, printer and word processing package for his/her school.

Second: £200, and a BBC computer and word processing package for his/her school.

Third: £100, and a BBC computer and word processing package.

There were six further national class prizes of £100. In addition regional winners received individual and school cash prizes and up to 1000 runners-up received special certificates of merit.

In 1989 the judges included Bill Cockburn (Royal Mail), Leonard Pagliero (Envelope Makers' and manufacturing Stationers' Association), Alan Tuffin (Union of Communication Workers) and Melanie McFadyean (Editor, Young Guardian).

The closing date for entries to the 1989 competition was 5th May 1989 and winners were announced in August.

Future: This is a regular annual competition with a different theme each year.

Entry: There is no entry form but the organisers do issue rules and conditions of entry. Among the requirements is that a teacher or parent/guardian must confirm that the letter is the entrant's own original work and that letters may be no longer than two sides of 'file paper'.

RTPI ANNUAL AWARD FOR PLANNING ACHIEVEMENT

The Royal Town Planning Institute, 26 Portland Place, London W1N 4BE
Telephone: 071 636 9107

Contact: David Fryer, Secretary General

This award, first made in 1978, is for outstanding group achievement in town and country planning in the British Isles. To merit the award the achievement must be a significant environmental improvement of lasting community benefit, or some other outstanding achievement judged to have advanced significantly the science and art of town planning for the benefit of the public.

The award will be for 'group, not individual, achievement and may be made to a planning team, planning firm, community group, local authority etc'. It is probably not generally recognised that this scheme is open to groups outside the professional planning sector, although in practice it would seem that few non local authority schemes are successful (or perhaps submitted in the first place).

The overall winner receives the RTPI Silver Jubilee Challenge Cup, which is held for a year, and a certificate which is retained. Other achievements may be presented with certificates at the discretion of judges.

In evaluating achievements the following criteria will be considered:

a) enhancement of the physical environment with recognisable social and economic benefit in terms of human happiness, safety and efficiency;

b) originality and innovation of the achievement or approach;

c) quality of professional work in design, development of planning concepts, and in application of planning techniques;

d) extent to which the scheme may serve as a model for work elsewhere or as a base for the development of further related schemes;

e) role played by the planner as an enabler and coordinator.

The size of a project is not necessarily relevant to the evaluation of an achievement.

The overall winner in 1989 was the London Planning Advisory Committee for its report: Strategic Planning Advice for London – Policies for the 1990s (this is the first time a report has been shortlisted). The London Docklands Development Corporation was highly commended for the redevelopment of Greenland Dock, and four entries were commended. These were the Market Place and associated priority pedestrian areas in Bolton, the Culver Centre in Colchester, the Brighter Islington Neighbourhood Security and Environmental Initiatives, and the Bridgwater-Taunton Canal project. Thirty-seven submissions were put forward by branches for national consideration of which ten were shortlisted.

The initial selection of projects for consideration by the national judges is coordinated by the local branches of the RTPI, through their Branch Executive Committees, who make their own arrangements. The scheme is publicised through The Planner journal and directly to Chief Planning Officers and RTPI branches. Branches may nominate up to five projects for consideration at national level. The national judges then consider these nominations and draw up a shortlist of projects for which more information may be requested or which may be visited.

The timetable appears to be the same each year and is as follows.

• Nominations must be notified to the appropriate local branch by 28th April.

• Nominations for consideration by the national judges must be submitted by 26th May.

Future: A well established scheme which we assume will continue. However the Judges' Report for 1988 remarked on the difficulty of judging a wide variety of types of projects and suggested that 'some simple rules might be devised for future years to make entries more readily comprehensible and comparable'.

RSPB BIRDS AND COUNTRYSIDE AWARDS

Royal Society for the Protection of Birds, The Lodge, Sandy, Bedfordshire SG19 2DL

Telephone: 0767 80551

Contact: Margaret Gaylor
Sponsor: Esso UK plc

This scheme, which ran from 1986 to 1989, is no longer continuing in its previous form. There will be no competition in 1990 but it is anticipated that a new scheme will be launched for 1991 aimed at young people. We do not know whether Esso UK will continue to be involved as sponsor. We have included brief information on the old scheme because it might give some indication of the nature of the new competition.

The Birds and Countryside Awards were for non-commercial organisations and individuals judged to have made the greatest collective contribution to wild bird and countryside conservation within the United Kingdom. In 1989 the awards were directed at projects involving young people from 9 to 16 years old in addition to categories for individuals, non-commercial bodies, industry and the media. In 1989 the overall winner received £1000 and there were two second prizes of £500.

The timetable for the 1989 awards required nominations/entries to be submitted by the end of March although the timetable for future schemes may be different.

Future: New scheme likely in 1991.

Entry: Previous competitions have required entries to be submitted on the official entry form together with supporting material.

RURAL EMPLOYMENT AWARD

Rural Development Commission (RDC), 141 Castle Street, Salisbury Wiltshire, SP1 3TP
Telephone: 0722 336255
Contact: Angela Turnbull, Press and Publicity Officer

Country Landowners Association, 16 Belgrave Square, London SW1
Telephone: 071 235 0511
Contact: Graham Downing

This scheme is organised jointly by the Rural Development Commission and the Country Landowners Association. Further information is probably best obtained from the former.

Launched in 1982 this annual award aims to encourage sustained employment by small businesses through the conversion of old buildings to new uses. Each year the competition focusses on a different region of England – in 1990 this will be the West of England. (The sequence is North, East, West and South, although there is some doubt as to whether this pattern and indeed the scheme itself will continue beyond 1990). There are no limitations on the types of business involved (provided it creates sustained non-agricultural employment), the number, size and type of buildings, or the type of tenure or business/landowner relationship.

Judges are particularly interested in the amount of new employment generated, the significance of that employment in the local community, and the extent to which the business and the building conversion reflect enterprise and initiative.

In 1989, 105 entries were received covering a very wide range of buildings and businesses. There were just 26 entries in 1982 when the scheme started and 67 in 1987. County winners receive a framed certificate and the overall regional winner receives £1000 and a brass plaque. Other awards may also be given. These include: The Best Runner-Up, The Project of Greatest Architectural Merit, and The Best Accomodation of High Technology Industry. The overall winner in 1988 was Country Holidays Ltd for its conversion of a disused cotton weaving mill to offices at Earby in Lancashire.

The competition is normally publicised in December with entries to be submitted by the end of the following February. Winners are announced and presented with their awards in June.

Future: Uncertain beyond 1990 in part because of structural reorganisation of the Rural Development Commission.

Entry: On the official entry form together with supporting documentation and photographs to be submitted to the RDC at the above address.

RURAL WALES AWARDS

Council for the Protection of Rural Wales, Ty Gwyn, 31 High Street, Welshpool, Powys SY21 7JP
Telephone: 0938 552525/556212

This annual scheme seeks to recognise work by individuals and organisations which is consciously intended to enhance the appearance or amenity of the countryside and by so doing to encourage others to follow these examples. Examples of eligible projects include: hedge-laying, restoring a stone wall, regeneration of indigenous woodland and tidying a derelict area. The scheme is open to individuals and voluntary, statutory and commercial organisations, although 'the primary intention is to encourage individual voluntary effort'.

The winners receive a framed certificate at local presentations. In 1988, 16 awards were presented for projects ranging from a new wildlife hide on a nature reserve, a road improvement scheme, conversion of private cottages and the restoration of several buildings of historic and architectural importance.

The local branches of CPRW select award winners. Each branch is encouraged to make at least two awards annually. The extent to which nominations for awards are actively sought will vary from branch to branch.

Nominations should be submitted to CPRW Head Office or local branches by the end of May each year.

Future: We assume that this scheme will continue.

Entry: Contact the local branch of CPRW (address from head office) for details of local arrangements.

SAINSBURY'S CHOIR OF THE YEAR COMPETITION

Kallaway Ltd, 2 Portland Road, Holland Park, London W11 4LA
Tel: 071 221 7883

Contact: Sarah Tenant-Flowers
Sponsor: J. Sainsbury plc

This competition was established in 1984, and has expanded and developed since then. It is now a major arts sponsorship project involving (in 1988) 300 choirs and several thousand individual singers. Sainsbury's state that their purpose in creating the competition was to 'provide a focal point for the choral movement'. It is organised on a biennial basis.

The competition is open to adult and youth amateur choirs from throughout the United Kingdom (which in this case embraces the Isle of Man). There is no restriction on the musical style – entries include church choirs, male, female and mixed voice choirs, chamber choirs, gospel choirs, madrigal groups, barbershoppers, and school choirs.

Entries are judged on the following criteria: musicianship, choral technique, programme choice and presentation. Choirs are judged on performed programmes which are left, within certain requirements on timing, to the discretion of the entrants themselves. However entrants are advised to adopt programmes which demonstrate their versatility and thus feature contrasting moods, styles and techniques, and to incorporate at least one piece written or arranged in the last fifty years.

The judging procedure for 1990 (which is similar but not identical to that adopted in 1988) is as follows:

Stage 1 (Audition): Audition Festival Days at centres throughout the UK. Places are limited and applications are dealt with in order of receipt.

Stage 2 (Selection): Thirty-two choirs (20 adult, 12 youth) are invited to take part on the basis of audition performances. This stage is held over one weekend in Horsham, Sussex and one weekend in Manchester.

Stage 3 (Finals): Twelve choirs (8 adult, 4 youth) selected from the Selection stage take part in the Finals Weekend. All perform on the Saturday with six finalists performing a second time on the Sunday. Winners are chosen from these finalists.

In 1990, the prizes were: £1750 and trophy for the overall winner – the Sainsbury's Choir of the Year; £1250 and a trophy for the Sainsbury's Youth Choir of the Year; and £250 to each of the losing finalists. Transport and accommodation costs for participation in Stages 2 and 3 are covered. Participants in all stages benefit from the advice of adjudicators and the opportunity to perform in front of a discerning audience and other competitors. The competition is normally covered by BBC Television and thus offers participants the opportunity of valuable media coverage.

For the 1990 competition, the closing date for entries was 31st January. The Stage 2 performances take place in October and the Stage 3 Finals Weekend in late November.

Future: The sponsors appear to be heavily committed to this competition and we assume it will continue for some time.

Entry: On the official entry form – at this stage choirs do not need to specify their intended performance programme. Detailed rules and requirements are issued with the entry form.

THE SANDFORD AWARD

Heritage Education Trust, St Mary's College, Strawberry Hill, Twickenham TW1 4SX

Telephone: 081 892 0051 ext. 202

Contact: Martin Dyer
Sponsor: Reed Information Services

The Heritage Education Trust aims to promote the educational use of historic properties by schools and to encourage owners and administrators of these properties to make special provision for educational groups. The Sandford Award is an important part of the Trust's work.

The organisers state that: 'the Award is open to any heritage site where the building itself and its contents or an historical garden or a traditional estate or an archaeological monument are used and experienced as an educational resource'. This definition opens the way for some, though not all, museums and galleries to be eligible.

Further advice on eligibility is available from the Trust. The Awards, which are of two types – full Sandford Awards and Highly Commended, are not competitive and may be made to any property where the educational services and facilities meet the criteria laid down by the Trust. The Awards take the form of a plaque. A major benefit of receiving an award is that winners are listed in the Reed Information Services guides: Museums and Galleries and Historic Houses Castles and Gardens. Being a 'Sandford Award Winner' can be a valuable promotional advantage for properties seeking to increase their income from educational groups. Award winners have to apply for 'quinquennial review' if they wish to remain listed as a Sandford Award Holder. Applications must relate to specific educational programmes and facilities and services for educational groups

The deadline for receipt of applications is 31st March annually. The 1989 awards were presented by Magnus Magnusson on 5th March 1990 at Culzean Castle and Country Park.

Future: A well established scheme which we assume will continue for some time.

Entry: By completed application form with supporting material including publicity handouts, educational material and two black and white photographs indicating educational aspects of the property.

The scheme is unusual in charging an entry fee. The standard fee (in 1989) was £75 although discounted fees (ranging between £10 and £30 depending on the number of visitors per year) are available to National Trust and National Trust for Scotland properties, properties in the care of the Department of the Environment and members of the Historic Houses Association and the Pilgrims Association.

SCANIA TRANSPORT TRUST AWARDS

Scania (Great Britain) Ltd and The Transport Trust are joint organisers and sponsors of this competition.

Scania (GB) Ltd, Tongwell, Milton Keynes, MK15 8HB
Telephone: 0908 215384.
Contact: Phil Sampson, Public Relations Officer

The Transport Trust, Melbury House, Melbury Terrace, London NW1 6JU
Telephone: 071 262 8864
Contact: The General Administrator

The Scania Transport Trust Awards which were launched in January 1988 are for projects which have contributed significantly to the preservation of transport heritage within the UK. One of the schemes main aims is to 'recognise the work being undertaken by the transport preservation movement in the UK'. The competition is open to all projects concerned with transport preservation, be they road, rail, water or air related. However the scheme will not cover the work of commercial restorers.

The organisation of the scheme is unusual, but appears to have been successful, for in its first year some 160 entries were received – over three times the number anticipated. The competition is run annually but spans two years. Entries (an entry form and supporting material) may be submitted at any time in the year – there is no closing date. These are then assessed and short-listed projects visited and judged. From these shortlisted projects up to four interim winners (or finalists) are identified three times a year – each receiving a cheque for £250. At the end of the year these finalists (a maximum of twelve per year) go through to the final assessment which decides the winners. The overall winner receives a specially commissioned trophy, a cheque and, along with runners-up, a 'VIP visit to Sweden to see some of the transport preservation projects in the Stockholm area and Scania's factory, museum and restoration workshop'. Other awards are at the discretion of the judges and the total value of the prizes is £10,000.

The overall winning projects in 1988/89 were the restoration of the Glasgow Paddle steamer Waverley, the Chatterley Whitfield Mining Museum (for a mining transport collection), the restoration of the world's last Fairey Gannet aircraft and Bristol's Industrial Museum (for the Steam Tug Mayflower).

Entries may be made at any time. The first national winners were announced in May 1989.

Future: Scania (GB) Ltd and The Transport Trust appear to be very committed to this competition judging by the quality and breadth of the supporting literature. We assume that this very new scheme will continue for some time.

Entry: On the official entry form. The submission of supporting material including photographs is welcome but is not a pre-condition of entry.

SCOTTISH MUSEUM OF THE YEAR AWARDS

c/o Scottish Museums Council, 20 Torpichen Street, Edinburgh, EH3 8JB
Telephone: 031 229 7465

Contact: The Countess of Perth

This scheme is distinct from the UK National Heritage Museum of the Year Awards (see separate entry in this book), entry for which must be made separately.

Awards under this scheme are made for 'the most significant additions or improvements to the museums and galleries of Scotland as centres for the preservation, study and interpretation of historical evidence and as enjoyable and instructive places to visit, having particular regard to the imaginative use of the resources available.' All museums and galleries owned either by a public or national authority or by a private trust are eligible. Entries should relate to 'recent developments'. The organisers give some examples of possible entries: a new museum, extension or reconstruction, display and interpretation, publications, audio-visual programmes, visitor facilities, educational services, research and conservation.

Temporary exhibitions at a single venue can only be considered exceptionally because of the difficulty of visiting.

The awards involve cash sums, although the number of awards and the amounts given are not specified in advance – they are given 'in relation to the resources of the museum as much as the quality of the entry'. In each year one or more entries are nominated for a Scottish Museum of the Year Award.

The closing date for entries is 31st May. Winners are announced (in Museums Bulletin and Scottish Museum News) about twelve months after the closing date for entries.

Future: We assume this scheme will continue.

Entry: On the official entry form together with a folder containing relevant photographs, press cuttings, brochures and other material.

SCOTTISH PLAYGROUND OF THE YEAR AWARDS

National Playing Fields Association (Scotland), 20 Queen Street, Edinburgh, EH2 1JX

Telephone: 031 225 4307

Contact: The Director

Sponsors; NPFA (Scotland), The Royal Town Planning Institute in Scotland, The Royal Incorporation of Architects in Scotland, The Landscape Institute in Scotland.

These awards aim to promote and encourage the planning and provision of facilities for children's play. The awards are open to local authorities, schools, organisations and any formal or informal groups. The scheme is run annually. The awards take the form of trophies, plaques, certificates and cash prizes but their exact nature and number are not specified by the organisers.

In the 1989 competition there were five categories of entry:

Section A: Provision of playgrounds in rural and urban areas

Section B: Low budget projects

Section C: School Grounds

Section D: Policy and Research

Section E: Playgrounds which integrate able-bodied and physically handicapped children.

Within Sections A, B and E judges look for:

• New or redesigned play areas where children's needs have been catered for as an integral part of the design (eg play spaces in housing areas or countryside parks).

• Design of play equipment, safe yet encouraging children to play and learn together.

• Proximity of facilities catering for other age groups.

• Design of equipment and site to ensure low maintenance costs and ease of access.

• Use of landscaping to integrate play area into physical environment.

Section C is based on a specific theme each year. In 1990 the award in this section will be for 'stimulating the enjoyment of environmental concerns within school grounds' and in 1991 for 'the development of a school wall or walls to promote and facilitate play'.

In Section D judges will consider:

• Adopted policies to increase the number and improve the quality of play areas.

• Criteria regarding the type, location and number of play areas.

• Research into the social/educational value of play.

• Monitoring use and responsiveness to change.

• Implementation and maintenance procedures possibly involving the local community and organisations.

Entries must relate to work done mainly in the year preceding entry.

The closing date for the 1989 awards was 31st July 1989 with the winners due to be announced in the late Autumn of that year.

Future: An established scheme which we assume will continue.

Entry: On the official entry form together with a proper location plan and if possible a portfolio of photographs.

SCOTTISH TOURISM AWARD

Perthshire Tourist Board, The Round House, Marshall Place, Perth PH2 8NU

Telephone: 0738 27958

Contact: John L Grainger, Secretary

Sponsors: Scottish Tourist Board and Stakis Hotels

This award, instituted in 1981, is for the Bill Heron Trophy and honours the late Bill Heron, one of the pioneers of Scottish Tourism. The Trophy is awarded annually to 'stimulate the flow of tourism ideas in Scotland' and is presented to the individual or organisation who has made 'the most significant contribution to Scottish tourism'. Entry is on the basis of nominations from third parties. There appear to be no restrictions (or guidelines) on the type of organisations or activities and achievements which can be rewarded.

In addition to the Bill Heron Trophy for the winner there is also a prize for the person who nominates the winner. In 1988 this was a return flight for two people from Scotland to London and two nights accomodation in a Stakis hotel in London. Previous recipients of the Trophy have included Dundee Heritage Trust (for RRS Discovery), Gordon District Tourist Board (for Scotland's Castle Trail), Scottish Television (for Take the High Road) and Dr Michael Kelly (ex Lord Provost of Glasgow).

The adjudication panel in 1989 was chaired by D Duncan Dewar (Managing Director, Best of Scotland Holidays) and included tourism officers from several local authorities and tourist boards. The closing date for nominations in 1989 was 22nd December.

Future: We assume this scheme will continue.

Entry: On the official nomination form – supporting material is welcomed.

SHELL BETTER BRITAIN CAMPAIGN

Red House, Hill Lane, Great Barr, Birmingham B43 6LZ (or Freepost Birmingham B43 5BR)

For Scotland: Balallan House, 24 Allan Park, Stirling FK8 2QG (or Freepost, Stirling FK8 2BR)

Contact: Peter Woodward, Director
Sponsor: Shell UK Ltd

The Shell Better Britain Campaign is probably one of the most sophisticated and well resourced commercially sponsored initiatives in the community action field. The Campaign has its origins in the Better Britain Competition established in 1970. The scheme has evolved and developed since – away from a recognition based competition to a major programme of advice and information giving and grant aid. The Campaign does offer a limited number of awards/prizes for outstanding achievement, but these are a relatively small part of the overall Campaign.

The scale of the Campaign is illustrated by the fact that in 1988 Shell committed £1 million to funding it over three years. It is also reflected in the involvement of the following major organisations as partners: Nature Conservancy Council, Countryside Commission, Countryside Commission for Scotland, British Trust for Conservation Volunteers, Scottish Conservation Projects Trust, Civic Trust, and Scottish Civic Trust.

The Campaign aims to 'help local voluntary and community groups do practical environmental and conservation projects of benefit to the community'. It has four main elements:

• Information – Mainly provided through the free 70 page book *Getting Help for Environmental Projects*. This publication contains ideas for projects, advice, and addresses of over 200 organisations able to provide further support.

• Advice – Specific problems not covered by the written information available can be dealt with through the provision of expert advice from the Campaign partners.

• Grants – £120,000 per year is available to local groups in grants of up to £500. The grants are not envisaged as total funding for a project but more for the provision of tools and raw materials, etc.

- **Awards** – In 1988 seven Best of Better Britain Awards (£250 in cash) were made to the most outstanding projects which had received a grant. In addition all projects which receive a grant and succeed in their original intentions receive a Campaign Achievement Certificate. Other specific awards, in 1988 The Wildwatch Award sponsored by Anglia TV and the Recycling Award, may also be offered.

The literature concerning the Campaign is clear and comprehensive. In brief the eligibility criteria for grant applications is as follows:

'Projects should result in a tangible improvement in the local community; involve a high proportion of voluntary effort from the local community; be of benefit to the wider community and not simply your own group; be properly thought out so that it will work.'

Within the overall grant fund there are specific allocations for recycling projects, for projects of direct benefit to wildlife conservation, and for projects related to improving the countryside and public enjoyment of it.

The Campaign publishes a booklet containing brief details of all the projects which received a grant award in the previous year. This should be extremely helpful to intending applicants. In 1988 there were 630 applications for grants – 366 were successful. The average grant was just under £300.

The procedure for seeking support from the Campaign is as follows. The first step is to request information on the Campaign. In return inquirers will receive the publications referred to above and a Grant Application Form. If a grant is required this form should be completed and returned. Each project for which a grant is requested is then visited personally by one of the eight Campaign Officers – all retired Shell employees. Grants are awarded on the basis of his/her report. Those in receipt of a grant are also expected to submit, within a year, a report on the project and it is in part on these reports that the recognition Awards are made.

Information and advice is available continuously, although in 1989 grant applications should have been made between May and the end of October.

Future: A very well established scheme which is certain to run until 1991 and no doubt for some years after.

Entry: Grant applications submitted on the official form with, if possible, two photographs of the site – slides or black and white prints.

SOUTH SOMERSET ENVIRONMENTAL AWARDS SCHEME

South Somerset District Council, PO Box 36, Council Offices, Brympton Way, Yeovil, Somerset, BA20 1DB
Telephone: 0935 75272

Contact: Alasdair Bell (ext 2420)

An annual scheme which was first launched in April 1989 to coincide with Environment Week. Awards are made to 'the best projects to improve the South Somerset environment'. Local schools, clubs, amenity groups and individuals resident in South Somerset are eligible to enter. The awards are in recognition of achievement. There are three categories of entry:

- the built environment (including improvements to buildings, derelict sites, wall murals; renovation of items of architectural interest etc);

- the natural environment (including improvements to sites such as ponds, rivers, parks, playing fields and unused land etc.);

- miscellaneous – any projects not in the other two categories.

Entries are judged by a panel comprising the Chairman of the Council and other councillors. In 1989 the prizes averaged about £100 each and six were awarded. We understand that more money might be available in 1990. The closing date for entries in 1990 is likely to be 9th June.

Future: The District Council intend to run this scheme every year.

Entry: There is no official entry form – all that is required is to send a description of the project (of no more than 250 words) to the above address.

STEAM HERITAGE AWARDS

Steam Heritage Awards, Hobart House, Grosvenor Place, London SW1X 7AE
Telephone: 071 235 2020

Contact: Mr A Mirchandaney/G R Ellard
Sponsor: British Coal

These annual awards are given in recognition of 'outstanding work by companies and organisations in the restoration and preservation of steam driven transport and machinery from a bygone age'. The competition embraces reclamation, restoration and conversion projects involving solid fuel for the generation of steam power.

There are four categories of entry relating to the following fields: rail, road, stationary engines and marine. The winner in each class receives an award of £750. The Premier Award, of £3000, is given to the project, from any of the categories, which demonstrates outstanding technical achievement.

In the 1989/90 scheme, the deadline for entries was 30th November 1989.

Future: We assume this scheme will continue.

Entry: On the official entry form which requires a brief description of the project. No advice on the submission of supporting material is offered.

TENNENT COMMUNITY AWARD

Tennent Caledonian Breweries Ltd, 110 Bath Street, Glasgow, G2 2ET
Telephone: 041 552 6552

Contact: Mr Nolan
Sponsor: Tennent Caledonian Breweries Ltd

We understand that the organisers/sponsors of this award do not publish any literature about the scheme nor appear actively to seek applications and nominations. The following, less than comprehensive information, is all we have been able to obtain.

The scheme, which has been run annually since 1981, aims to encourage groups to show initiative in improving and preserving their local environment, although on the basis of the 1987 winner (the Biggar Museum Trust for the re-creation of a Victorian street within the museum) this criteria seems to be interpreted fairly liberally. Any voluntary group in Scotland is eligible for an award. There appears to be one overall winner each year, which receives a cash award. In 1989, this was for £3000 and went to the Fife Folk Museum in Ceres.

We understand that nominations are made and considered by a committee comprising representatives of the company and the Scottish Civic Trust. This committee meets three times a year to consider nominations, visits shortlisted schemes and then selects the overall winner.

Future: We assume this scheme will continue.

Entry: Nominations are made by members of the Award Committee themselves.

THEAKSTON HERITAGE FUND

Theakston Heritage Fund, Visitor's Centre, T & R Theakston Ltd. The Brewery, Masham, North Yorkshire, HG4 4DX

Telephone: 031 225 9587

Contact: Linda Melville

This new scheme, launched in mid 1989, provides grants for environmental projects. Although not strictly a competition, as the grants are for the implementation of projects rather than in recognition of achievement, we have included details in this book partly because as a consequence of the schemes newness there is little information on it readily available. Furthermore the operation of the scheme (one deadline for entries, judging procedure, selection of finalists, presentation of 'awards', etc.) embraces some of the elements of a 'competition'.

The scheme is designed to help and encourage individuals and groups to preserve, enhance or improve their environment, especially the rural environment. Anyone over 18 living in the United Kingdom may apply as an individual or on behalf of a group. The following conditions apply:

- the project's prime purpose must be to conserve, enhance or improve the environment;
- the project has not received grant support from any other source;
- the project does not involve works which are a requirement of planning permission or tree preservation orders;
- official approvals and consents must have been obtained;
- tree or shrub species are appropriate to the landscape and the needs of agriculture, will benefit wildlife conservation and will establish successfully;
- there is no objection to the project being publicised in the event of a grant being awarded.

Projects in receipt of an award must be completed within twelve months of the grant offer.

Examples of projects which could be eligible include: a city farm, rejuvenating woodland, tree planting, restoring a pond and signing a nature walk.

The total fund available in 1989 was £30,000 (£15,000 from Theakston, £12,000 from the Countryside Commission and £3000 from the Countryside Commmission for Scotland). Grants are anticipated to be in the range £500 to £5000, but will be 'kept small to encourage those voluntary projects that would not normally qualify for existing funding from local government or from charitable organisations'.

In 1989 the deadline for applications was 31st October. Selection, which can involve site inspections, took place in November, successful applicants notified in December and awards presented in January 1990. Grants are awarded by an independent panel which includes leading environmentalists.

Future: We assume that all the partners to this scheme will wish to continue their involvement if the first year of operation is seen to be a success.

Entry: On the official application form with 'as much supporting information as possible' including if possible a colour photograph of the site.

THE THF COMMUNITY CHEST

The Conservation Foundation, 1 Kensington Gore, London SW7 2AR
Telephone: 071 823 8842

Contact: None given
Sponsor: Trusthouse Forte

Strictly speaking The THF Community Chest is more akin to a grant fund than a competition in the sense that it provides help to projects planned or in progress rather than completed. The principle behind the scheme is that 'everyone can take an active part in improving, conserving and preserving the environment'. It aims to 'assist projects which help communities to improve and enjoy their local environment... No project is to big or small to enter'.

Each month up to £1800 is offered in grants to projects throughout the UK on the basis of submitted applications. The total of grants over the year is currently £20,000 with individual grants ranging from £200 to £1000. Twenty-two projects were awarded grants in 1988 including a church tower restoration, an urban wildlife group, a landscaping scheme and a wildflower garden.

Entries are acknowledged upon receipt by The Conservation Foundation who send the entrant an entry number. Applications are then judged by an independent panel of judges, headed by the ubiquitous David Bellamy. Those awarded a grant are notified and put in touch with a local Trusthouse Forte representative who will help organise a local presentation of the cheque, possibly by a well known personality.

One advantage of this scheme over competitions is that there is no timetable entrants need to adhere to – application may be made at any time.

Future: We assume that the scheme will remain in existence for some time.

Entry: On the official (and very simple) application form with supporting material (eg photographs) if desired. Forms should be available at THF hotels and restaurants (including Harvesters, Wheelers, Little Chef, Happy Eater and Gardner Merchant), Welcome Break Service Areas, and Lillywhites, as well as from The Conservation Foundation.

TIMES/PM ENVIRONMENT AWARD

The Times, PO Box 486, 1 Pennington Street, London E1 9XN
Telephone: 071 580 4468

Contact: Michael Hoy
Sponsors: The Times/ BBC Radio (PM Programme on Radio 4).

This award, launched in 1989, is aimed at individuals, groups and communities who have made a significant contribution to improving their local environment or the environment in general. It is particularly designed to promote the value of practical physical schemes such as safeguarding or restoring threatened or damaged countryside, preserving wildlife habitats, reducing pollution, waste recycling and energy conservation. Campaigns, which can demonstate their impact in a defined area, and educational initiatives are also eligible.

The scheme is open to projects in the United Kingdom which have been active in the preceding year. Professionals and local authorities, as well as individuals and voluntary groups, may enter, but they must demonstrate work and initiative extending well beyond their regular duties. The winner receives a commemorative trophy, extensive national publicity and £5000 to be spent on furthering the project in consultation with the organisers.

In 1989, nominations/entries had to be submitted by 3rd February 1989.

A shortlist of five entries is chosen and these projects are featured in The Times and on the PM programme later in February. Readers and listeners then chose the winner which is announced the following month on PM and in The Times. Judges in 1989 included Stanley Clinton Davis (ex EC Environment Minister), Professor James Lovelock FRS and the environment correspondents and editors of The Times and PM programme.

Future: The organisers intend to continue the competition in 1990.

Entry: Nominations of up to 250 words to the above address including photographs if possible. There is no official entry form.

THE TIMES/RIBA COMMUNITY ENTERPRISE SCHEME

RIBA, 66 Portland Place, London W1N 4AD
Telephone: 071-580-5533

Contact: Administrator, Community Enterprise Scheme
Sponsors: The Times, Royal Institute of British Architects and Business in the Community. Supported (in 1988/89) by The Calouste Gulbenkian Foundation, The Community Projects Foundation and The National Children's Play and Recreation Unit.

The Scheme is '..an annual award for the most imaginative, viable and need-fulfilling community projects in the United Kingdom. The aim is to encourage community initiatives of all kinds where local enthusiasm and drive has been advanced with the support and assistance of community architects and other members of the environmental professions.'

'Any community initiated building project is eligible and this includes new housing self-help/self-build, housing association work, refurbishment and renovation projects, community centres [and village halls], adventure playgrounds, urban farms, small business workshops, environmental improvements and facilities and improvements for the disabled'. Special emphasis is placed on the degree of community involvement in the initiation and development of a project and on the process by which it has reached its present stage.

Projects should be in the process of being developed or built, and should have passed the feasibility stage at the time of entry. Whenever possible a feasibility study should accompany the entry.

Any member of the community may enter including individuals, community organisations, local authorities, schools and businesses.

In 1988/89 the Community Projects Foundation sponsored a special award for schemes embodying successful and creative partnerships in community regeneration, and the Childrens's Play and Recreation Unit sponsored special awards for community initiated play projects involving the built environment. These special awards may not continue in future years although the principle of involving other organisations in particular types of awards within the overall scheme is well established.

Entries are assessed initially by an eighteen strong panel chaired by John Thompson, President of RIBA, and including including several people themselves active in local projects. Projects shortlisted then go forward to a second stage which involves visits. Shortlisted projects may feature in The Times during the assessment period. Award winning projects receive a cash prize and a plaque and can reasonably expect to be featured in a Special Report in The Times to coincide with the Awards Presentation.

A total of £14,000 was available for winners in 1988/89. The top three were the Community Action in the Rural Environment (CARE) project in Barnsley, Antur Waunfawr – a charitable company set up to 'bring handicapped people into village life and to encourage them to develop their full potential', and West Walker Community Development's project to involve local children in Newcastle upon Tyne in determining the future of their primary school.

Seven other projects received major awards and a further 25 were commended. There were over 300 entries in all.

The timetable for the 1989/90 Scheme required entries to be submitted by 7th March 1990. Projects completed before this date are not eligible. The 1989 awards were presented by HRH The Prince of Wales on 27th June 1989.

Future: There are likely to be some changes to the Scheme including different organisations as partners although the basic format will stay the same. In 1990/91, nine categories are eligible for Awards: the Housing Associations' Charitable Trust Award for housing; the Times Environmental Award; the Gulbenkian Awards for workplaces and for community centres; the Community Projects Foundation Award for partnership; the National Children's Play Award; the Community Architecture Award; and the Community Enterprise Awards for training and for new business. The Scheme has been so successful that at the time of writing a full-time Administrator was due to be appointed.

Entry: On the official entry form. Entrants are also encouraged to submit photographs, a location plan, and feasibility study.

TOMORROW'S NEW COMMUNITIES COMPETITION

Town and Country Planning Association (TCPA), 17 Carlton House Terrace, London SW1Y 5AS

Telephone: 071 930 8903/4/5

Contact: David Hall, Director
Sponsor/Partner: The Joseph Rowntree Memorial Trust. Supported also by Capital and Counties plc.

This is a new competition due to be launched in January 1990. It is designed to 'stimulate fresh thinking about new forms of development that will provide a better quality of living environment to meet the needs of the next century, and to improve development practice'. The organisers see the competition as an opportunity to 'design new forms of settlement which will have the success and the world-wide influence of the early garden cities, setting new standards of balanced development in which the quality of life and adequate funding of community facilities are both essential ingredients'.

The competition is for designs/proposals for new communities in the following categories:

1. A village or group of hamlets or new form of mixed urban and rural development for a population of up to 3000.

2. A small free-standing town in the range of 12,000 to 18,000 people.

3. An expansion of about 10,000 people added to an existing town.

In categories 1 and 2 the site may include a small existing settlement or settlements not exceeding 10% of the total population of the proposed settlement. Entry is open to any organisation or individual of whatever nationality although entries must relate to specific UK sites. The organisers hope the competition will attract both professionals and interested amateurs. Student entries are invited and will be judged separately (in a separate category 4) in each of the three categories above. The first, second and third prizes in Categories 1, 2 and 3 will be £1500, £1000 and £500 and in Category 4 (students) £500, £350 and £150. The organisers have plans for a major exhibition of winning entries and are considering producing a television programme to link with the competition.

Judges will be influenced by the manner in which entries incorporate or have regard to the following:

• A physical design which reflects human scale in an attractive environment and which allows ease of access within the settlement and to and from elsewhere.

• A mixture of land uses appropriate to the size and locational context of the development, including an appropriate mix of housing types and tenures; employment, recreational and cultural opportunities; community services and facilities; and having regard to realistic demographic and economic conditions.

• The principles of sustainable development.

• The assembly of land together with assumptions as to ownership, price, phasing of development and subsequent management.

• The potential of the principles and practices to be more widely applied.

• The carrying out of the development by an appropriate agency or agencies and the subsequent role of such agencies after completion.

This is not an exhaustive list – judges will look for 'imagination and innovation in all aspects of the planning, design, implementation and on-going management of the settlement'.

The closing date for 1990 submissions is 30th September 1990. Queries about the terms and conditions of entry should be made before 31st July. No scheme, the design of which commenced before 1st January 1989 will be eligible.

Future: We assume that this competition is a one-off although we expect the TCPA to continue to be active in promoting the concept and practice of 'new communities'.

Entry: Entries should comprise designs, a report containing supporting material and one model or audio/visual presentation. Full details of the entry procedure will be available from TCPA.

TREES FOR PEOPLE: ARBORETUM COMPETITION

Trees for People Trust, 141 London Road, St Albans, Herts AL1 1TA
Telephone: 0727 67196

Contact: Simon Klinger, Director

The competition is open to all schools and youth organisations in the United Kingdom willing to create a new arboretum on not less than 1/2 acre. Although the scheme offers 'prizes' it is quite clear that these are offered to help implement proposed projects and not in recognition of achievement.

The prizes are as follows: First: £1000, Second: £500, Third: £250. There are unspecified consolation prizes for five further projects. The whole of the prize money must be spent on the proposed projects and proof of this must be submitted. Winners are required to give formal guarantees that their project will be implemented with immediate effect and completed within two years. They will also be requested to guarantee the upkeep of their project for at least five years. Guarantees from local authorities and/or school governors are essential, especially regarding long-term maintenance and protection of the land against future development. Entrants are urged to seek professional advice from landscapers, arborists and their local authorities.

Entries must be submitted by 1st December (extended from 1st October) for consideration and adjudication in the following three months.

Future: This is an annual competition which we assume will continue.

Entry: There is no entry form. Submissions (in triplicate) should include detailed designs and layouts and include site plans, photographs and details of tree and shrub species to be planted.

T.S. SHIPMAN PRIZE

University of Technology, Loughborough, Leicestershire, LE11 3TU
Telephone: 0509 263171

Contact: Dr B P Vale, Secretary to Prizes Committee.

This award is presented annually by the University to a registered student (of the University, Loughborough College or Loughborough College of Art and Design) or group of students who has or have contributed most to the development of co-operation between the University or Colleges and the local community. The main objective of the Award is to 'recognise activities which would lead to the improvement of the situation of groups of people or individuals in Loughborough and the surrounding villages'. Voluntary work not concerned with people but of benefit to the community is eligible.

Awards are judged on the basis of submitted nominations by third parties. Previous award winners have been involved with: Charnwood Stroke Club, the District Handicapped Children's Group, the Shelthorpe Hearts Football Club, local Guide and Brownie Groups, and a drama workshop for the visually handicapped. Two awards are offered each year, of £100 and £50.

In 1989 nominations were invited during the Spring term.

Future: An annual prize which we assume will continue.

Entry: On the basis of nominations which should include a brief synopsis of the nature of the work undertaken, its results and the period of involvement.

TSW SHOOTFIRST AWARD

Television South West, Derry's Cross, Plymouth, PL1 2SP
Telephone: 0752 663322

This award, launched in 1989, is for independent film-makers and artists working with video. It is open to individuals and groups within the TSW transmission area (Cornwall and Isles of Scilly,

Devon and parts of Somerset and Dorset) with a 'programme idea'. It is relevant to voluntary groups and charities because programme ideas could relate to their own activities and campaigns.

Shootfirst provides funding for the development and eventual production of a programme proposal from the independent grant-aided film sector. The scheme seeks programme ideas that are of regional relevance and show a genuine innovative approach. Likely themes for programmes are current affairs, community issues and documentaries. Drama and possibly animation are unlikely to be supported because of their high cost.

The application procedure is as follows. Entrants first submit a brief synopsis (up to two sides of A4) of their programme idea. From this submission a shortlist of up to five programme ideas are selected and a budget (of £200) provided for the preparation of a full treatment, story board if appropriate, and budget. From these proposals one project is selected and commissioned for production. TSW provide the winner with a realistic budget 'broadly equivalent to a local half hour 'above the line' budget at TSW. TSW are closely involved throughout the production process.

In 1989 the deadline for the submission of initial ideas was the end of July. Full treatments had to be submitted by the end of August and the final commission was announced in September. Three months was allowed for production and the final programme was expected to be shown in TSW's Winter 89/90 schedule.

Future: Uncertain – probably dependent on the success of the first scheme in 1989.

Entry: As outlined above. Full details should be obtained from TSW at the above address.

TUNSTALL TELECOM NATIONAL CARING AWARDS

Tunstall Telecom, Freepost, Whitley Bridge, Yorkshire, DN14 0BR
Telephone: 0979 661234

Contact: Ms Sharon Carroll
Sponsor: Tunstall Telecom

This award scheme, in its ninth year in 1989, is designed to give recognition to the efforts of all those individuals and organisations who, through vocation or profession, devote time and effort to lighten and brighten the lives of elderly people and people with disabilities.

There are two awards, one for individuals and one for organisations.

The Individual Award winner receives a holiday of his/her choice up to the value of £1000. All individual finalists receive a cut glass rose bowl and everyone nominated receives an inscribed certificate.

The Organisation Award winner receives £5000 to be spent on a nominated project which aims to make the lives of those being cared for more enjoyable and fulfilling.

The basis of the Individual Award is to recognise 'someone who deserves reward for remarkable care and devotion' given to elderly or disabled people. Nominations are invited for people who have 'voluntarily or professionally given outstanding service to the care and well-being of elderly people or those with disabilities who need special attention'. The Organisation Award is for projects which would make the lives of elderly and disabled people more enjoyable and fulfilling. The scope of such projects is very wide. Some examples are: equipping a new facility such as rest room or gym, an item of special equipment, a minibus or a special trip or event.

Previously unsuccessful nominations and applications in both categories may be resubmitted. All entries are examined by a panel of judges. The closing date for nominations and applications in 1989 was 31st August. The presentation luncheon took place in the Autumn in York.

Future: We assume that this well established scheme will continue.

Entry: Both nominations (for the Individual Award) and applications (for the Organisation Award) are made on the same official form. Supporting material (not specified) may be submitted.

TV-AM CARING CHRISTMAS SCHOOLS COMPETITION

TV-AM, Hawley Crescent, London, NW1 8EF
Telephone: 071 267 7072

Contact: Penny Mansergh

This award is open to schools throughout the United Kingdom. The organisers do not specify the aim or purpose of the competition but it is clearly designed to demonstrate the care shown to elderly people by school children. The competition is organised in partnership with almost 100 local/regional newspapers.

Schools are invited to prepare a short (under 10 minute) video film depicting a particular 'caring' activity or project undertaken by the school. Examples given include: a carol concert, nativity play or other performance, making or taking a gift to an elderly person, filling a Christmas hamper for an elderly person or 'something else which helps makes Christmas better for elderly people'.

The entry procedure is as follows. Schools should register their intention to enter by submitting a completed form to the Promotions Manager of their nearest participating newspaper. Entrants then submit their completed video to the same newspaper. Selected videos then go forward to a regional final – each regional finalist receives a six-pack of video films. Finalists are announced on TV-AM. The thirteen finalists are then judged, with the best three shown on TV-AM. A viewers' telephone poll then determines the overall winner.

The winning school receives a trophy, video camera, video recorder and television and a stack of tapes all donated by Boots. Two hundred of the school's students get a day-trip to Blackpool and the two runners-up receive small replicas of the trophy and a pack of videos.

In 1989 videos had to be submitted by 4th December.

Future: No information available.

Entry: As detailed above. Initial registration to participating newspaper on simple entry form.

TWIN TOWN AWARDS

c/o The Quentin Bell Organisation, 22 Endell Street, Covent Garden, London WC2H 9AD

Telephone: 071 379 4732

Contact: Lotte Irwin/Ina Foley
Sponsors: Royal Mail International/The Sunday Times

This scheme was first launched (in The Sunday Times) in June 1989.

Its stated purpose is 'to increase awareness of twinned towns and their activities and to encourage further twinning initiatives'.

The Awards are for the best twinning programmes involving events, exchanges, business links, projects and other activities. There are six categories of entry:

1. Culture – evidence of increased understanding of the entrants 'twin' and cultural exchanges where twin towns have mutually benefitted will be important.

2. Sport (eg sporting exchanges)

3. Education (eg increased comunication on education systems)

4. Commerce (eg better understanding of commercial activities)

5. Environment – initiatives which examine environmental issues and activities will be looked for.

6. International communication (eg through increased correspondence)

Entries must relate to activities undertaken after January 2nd 1988 (for the 1989 Awards) and may involve one or more twinning arrangements. Entry is open to any twinned village, town or city. Differences in size and population are taken into account by the judges.

The Grand Award winner, whose overall twinning programme is judged most successful across all the above category areas, receives a cheque for £1000 and £5000 in Royal Mail Aerogrammes. Framed certificates are awarded for outstanding performances in the individual categories. Entries are judged by a panel of representatives from the sponsors and the Joint Twinning Committee and other prominent figures.

The 1989 competition required entries to be submitted by 30th October 1989. Awards were presented at a gala luncheon in London in December and published in The Sunday Times.

Future: We understand that the sponsors hope to continue the scheme in future years.

Entry: On the official entry form with a description of the programme (maximum 500 words) and supporting material such as photographs, cuttings and proposals.

VILLAGE HALL AWARDS

Further information:
Rural Community Councils (all are listed in the entry on Village Ventures in this book).

or ACRE, Stroud Road, Cirencester, Glos GL7 6JR
Telephone: 0285 653477

Sponsors: Various.

Several Rural Community Councils (RCCs) organise a county competition to find and publicise the 'best' village halls in their area. Most of these competitions are designed to promote good upkeep and effective use of halls. Some focus on the 'best kept' while others are concerned with the overall management of halls. Prizes generally include cash awards in addition to trophies and plaques. The competitions are most developed in the South West of England where the RCCs (in Devon, Cornwall, Avon and Somerset) have organised a regional competition for the county winners. We are also aware of Village Hall Competitions in Cambridgeshire, Northamptonshire and Hereford and Worcester and Suffolk.

Future: We expect the number of Village Hall competitions to increase although in some counties there is a slight hiatus as a new sponsor, to replace Girobank which withdrew at the beginning of 1989, is sought. If a suitable sponsor can be found then a national competition or further regional competitions may be organised.

Entry: Entry criteria and procedure, timetable and the nature of the awards will vary from county to county. Contact ACRE or individual RCCs for details.

VILLAGE VENTURES

In every shire county in England and some in Wales there is a Village Ventures Competition organised by the county Rural Community Council.

Although the actual titles vary (for example the Clwyd Local Endeavour Competition, Kent Enterprizes, Surrey Village Initiative Prizes) all have the same basic objectives and are organised in a similar way.

The names and phone numbers of the county organisers are listed below. If you have difficulty contacting your RCC then get in touch with ACRE – the national association of Rural Community Councils at:

ACRE, Stroud Road, Cirencester, Glos. GL7 6JR
Tel: 0285 653477

Sponsors: All English competitions are sponsored by the Rural Development Commission and the vast majority by Shell UK Ltd which has been an active supporter of these schemes since their inception.

Village Ventures Competitions aim to encourage and support self-help projects undertaken by voluntary groups and organisations in rural areas. Awards are generally in recognition of projects which have been completed rather than for proposals or ideas. The competitions are intended to demonstrate and promote the potential and achievements of rural community action and thereby to inspire others. They are open to all kinds of projects – social, environmental, cultural and economic. Village hall improvement and re-building schemes, play projects, environmental improvement, community transport services, sports facilities and local newsletters are common entries but there are normally very few restriction on eligibility. Some competitions offer a special award for a particular type of project, such as village newsletters, which the RCC is keen to encourage. This may vary from year to year.

Most but not all competitions are run every other year but they all operate to different timetables. So if you are interested then make sure you get in touch with the relevant county organiser as soon as possible – they will put you on a mailing list if information is not immediately available.

The awards themselves vary from county to county but most involve a cash prize and some form of trophy, plaque or certificate. The Wiltshire competition for example offers a first prize of £500, two second prizes of £250, three third prizes of £125, and all entrants receive a Certificate of Merit.

A major benefit of these competitions is that they help those who enter to become more aware of the advice and other forms of help available from the RCC and other organisations. In many competitions all entrants are visited by a member of the staff of the RCC – this face-to-face contact can be very valuable to both parties. In addition most RCCs operate Rural Initiative Funds providing small grants and/or interest free loans to community projects. Entry to a Village Ventures Competition may help you to get access to this source of help.

Future: Both major sponsors and the RCCs themselves seem committed to continuing and where possible developing Village Ventures Competitions. In 1984 national awards were made to the most innovative projects submitted from the county competitions but there is at present no intention to repeat this in the near future.

Entry: Normally on the official entry form with supporting material to the relevant county organiser.

County Organisers:

Avon: Avon Community Council, 209 Redland Road, Bristol BS6 6YU Tel: 0272 736822

Bedfordshire: Bedfordshire Rural Community Council, The Old School, Southill Road, Cardington, Bedford, MK44 3SX Tel: 0234 838 771/2

Berkshire: Community Council for Berkshire, Epping House, 55 Russell Street, Reading, RG1 7XG Tel: 0734 566556

Buckinghamshire: Buckinghamshire Council for Voluntary Service, Walton House, Walton Street, Aylesbury, Bucks HP21 7QQ Tel: 0296 21036

Cheshire: Cheshire Community Council, 96 Lower Bridge Street, Chester CH1 1RU Tel: 0244 322188/323602

Cleveland: Cleveland Council for Voluntary Service, 47 Princes Road, Middlesborough, Cleveland TS1 4BG Tel: 0642 240651/2

Cornwall: Cornwall Rural Community Council, 9A River Street, Truro, Cornwall TR1 2RS Tel: 0872 73952

Cumbria: Cumbria Council for Voluntary Action, Birbeck House, Duke Street, Penrith, Cumbria CA11 7NA Tel: 0768 68086

Derbyshire: Derbyshire Rural Community Council, Church Street, Wirksworth, Derby DE4 4EY Tel: 062982 4797

Devon: Community Council for Devon, County Hall, Topsham Road, Exeter EX2 4QD Tel: 0392 77977

Dorset: Dorset Community Council, 57 High West Street, Dorchester DT1 1UT Tel: 0305 62270

Durham: Durham Rural Community Council, Aykley Heads, Durham DH1 5UN Tel: 09138 43511

Essex: Rural Community Council for Essex, 79 Springfield Road, Chelmsford CM2 6JG Tel: 0245 352046

Gloucestershire: Gloucestershire Rural Community Council, Community House, 15 College Green, Gloucester GL1 2LZ Tel: 0452 28491 (Gloucestershire RCC also runs an Urban Ventures competition along similar lines to the rural scheme.)

Hampshire: Hampshire Council of Community Service, Beaconsfield House, Andover Road, Winchester SO22 6AT Tel: 0962 54971

Hereford and Worcester: Hereford & Worcester Rural Community Council, Room 225, County Buildings, St Mary's Street, Worcester WR1 1TN Tel: 0905 22384

Hertfordshire: Community Council for Hertfordshire, 2 Townsend Avenue, St Albans AL1 3SG Tel: 0727 52298

Humberside: Community Council of Humberside, 14 Market Place, Howden, Goole, N. Humberside DN14 7BJ Tel: 0430 430904

Isle of Wight: Isle of Wight Rural Community Council, 42 The Mall, Carisbrook Road, Newport, IoW Tel: 0983 524058

Kent: Kent Rural Community Council, 15 Manor Road, Folkestone, CT20 2AH Tel: 0303 850816

Lancashire: Community Council of Lancashire, 15 Victoria Road, Fulwood, Preston PR2 4PS Tel: 0772 717461

Leicestershire: Leicestershire Rural Community Council, Community House, 133 Loughborough Road, Leicester LE4 5LX Tel: 0533 662905

Lincolnshire: Community Council of Lincolnshire, 1 Kesteven Street, Sleaford NG34 7DT Tel: 0529 302466

Norfolk: Norfolk Rural Community Council, 20 Market Place, Hingham, Norfolk NR9 4AF Tel: 0953 851408

Northamptonshire: Northamptonshire Rural Community Council, Hunsbury Hill Centre, Harksome Hill, Northampton NN4 9QX Tel: 0604 765888

Northumberland: Community Council of Northumberland, Tower Buildings, 9 Oldgate, Morpeth NE61 1PT Tel: 0670 517178

Nottinghamshire: Nottinghamshire Rural Community Council, Minster Chambers, Church Street, Southwell NG25 0HD Tel: 0636 815267

Oxfordshire: Oxfordshire Rural Community Council, The Hadow Rooms, 101 Banbury Road, Oxford OX2 6NE Tel: 0865 512488

Shropshire: Community Council for Shropshire, 1 College Hill, Shrewsbury SY1 1LT Tel: 0743 60641

Somerset: Community Council for Somerset, St Margaret's, Hamilton Road, Taunton TA1 2EG Tel: 0823 331222/3

Staffordshire: Community Council of Staffordshire, St George's, Corporation Street, Stafford ST16 3AG Tel: 0785 42525

Suffolk: Community Council for Suffolk, Alexandra House, Rope Walk, Ipswich IP4 1LZ Tel: 0473 230000

Surrey: Surrey Voluntary Service Council, Jenner House, 2 Jenner Road. Guildford GU1 3PN Tel: 0483 66072

Sussex (East and West): Sussex Rural Community Council, Sussex House, 212 High Street, Lewes BN7 2NH Tel: 0273 473422

Warwickshire: Warwickshire Rural Community Council, The Abbotsford, 10 Market Place, Warwick CV34 4SL Tel: 0926 499596

Wiltshire: Community Council for Wiltshire, Wyndhams, St Joseph's Place, Bath Road, Devizes SN10 1DD Tel: 0380 2475

Yorkshire: Yorkshire Rural Community Council, William House, Skipton Road, Skelton, York YO3 6WZ Tel: 0904 645271

Clwyd: Clwyd Voluntary Services Council, Ffordd yr Orsaf, Rhuthun, Clwyd LL15 1BP Tel: 082 42 2441/3805

Dyfed: Dyfed Association of Voluntary Services, 11/12 King Street, Carmarthen, Dyfed SA31 1BH Tel: 0267 236367

VPB DESIGN AWARD FOR INTERPRETIVE PANELS

Society for the Interpretation of Britain's Heritage
c/o 4 Holmewood Close, Kenilworth, Warwickshire CV8 2JE

Contact: Ian Parkin
Sponsor: VPB Industries

This scheme operates within the overall framework of the Gateway Interpret Britain Awards (see separate entry), although the VPB Award does have its own entry form and criteria.

The purpose of the VPB Design Award is to recognise and publicise outstanding design in the visual layout and presentation of interpretive (wayside) panels. The award relates to any interpretive panel erected for the benefit of visitors anywhere in the United Kingdom (including Orkney, Shetland, the Isle of Man and the Channel Islands). Entries may be submitted by the designer, promoter or the person or organisation who owns it and is responsible for its care. The entry can be a single panel or a series within the same overall theme. They may be interpretive or primarily orientational. Judges look for panels which: communicate effectively and unambiguously; are easy to read and understand; are appealing and welcoming; and fit the purpose for which they were designed. There are three cash prizes (£150, £75 and £25).

The timetable is identical to that for the Gateway Interpret Britain Awards. In 1989, 13th May was the deadline for entries and awards were due to be presented in January 1990 although normally awards would be presented in the calendar year of the competition.

Future: We assume this scheme will continue as long as the sponsor remains committed to it. We understand that sponsorship for 1990 has not yet been confirmed although the organisers are optimistic.

Entry: On the official form with a location plan, the detailed design of the panel and four A5 unmounted photographs.

WAINWRIGHT ACHIEVEMENT AWARD

Kendal Town Council, Town Hall, Kendal, Cumbria, LA9 4DQ
Telephone: 0539 733333 ext 496 or 0539 727828

Contact: Percy Duff, Town Treasurer

This award was established in 1989 to recognise the individual or organisation which 'has done most in the previous year to promote the prestige of Kendal or contributed significantly to the betterment of its inhabitants'. The first award is due to be made in January 1990.

The award was established by Alfred Wainwright who donated £10,000 to a trust, the sole function of which is to provide funds for the annual award. The trust deed stipulates that no single award shall exceed £500 (or other sum determined by the trustees), that in any year an award may not be given if there is no candidate of sufficient merit, and that political activity is not eligible. The trustees are the Town Mayor and Councillors of Kendal Town Council.

Future: The award is intended to be offered annually and on the basis of the trust established for the purpose will continue.

Entry: The organisers intend to insert an advertisement in The Westmorland Gazette annually in December, inviting nominations to be submitted to the Town Council.

WHITBREAD VOLUNTEER ACTION AWARDS
(formerly the Whitbread Community Care Awards)

Harrison Cowley Public Relations, King William House, 13 Queen Square, Bristol, BS1 4NT

Telephone: 0272 292311

Contact: Sally Burrows
Sponsor: Whitbread and Company plc in association with The Volunteer Centre UK

We understand that the title of this scheme will shortly be changed.

The Awards are 'designed to discover and reward the unsung heroes and heroines in British society...people who, through their own care and concern, provide comfort and support for others in the community'. Awards are open to individuals and groups although the bulk of the 2000 or so nominations (in 1989) and eventual winners are individuals. People are nominated for awards by others.

The official nomination form for the 1990 Award provides the following guidelines on the type of activities the scheme seeks to encourage:

• Voluntary work, involving help for individuals disadvantaged by age, physical or mental handicap, sickness or lack of knowledge or experience.

• Work for the benefit of the community by contributing to the improvement of local facilities.

• Involvement of young people directly or indirectly with service to themselves or other groups.

• Personal sacrifice of an individual or group to support less fortunate members of the community.

• Raising money for worthwhile projects within the community.

Careful reading of these guidelines reveals the breadth of the scheme which perhaps the former title "Community Care" did not adequately reflect.

In 1990 there will be nine regional winners each receiving a cash award of £1000 – £500 towards the cause and £500 to be spent at the winner's discretion.

There will also be a national UK Winner selected from the regional winners, who received £2000. In addition there is a national Young Person of the Year Award of £1000 open to anyone under the age of 24. Also certificates are presented on a regional basis to a number of nominations whom the judges feel should be highly commended.

The 1988 winners included Reg Hoskins who has been showing films to patients in the spinal injuries unit of a local hospital for the past 33 years, a Multiple Sclerosis sufferer who helped to set up a local branch of the MS Society and raise funds for a residential home for MS sufferers; and the Croydon Befrienders Scheme set up to help young people who are in trouble with the police or at risk of getting into trouble.

The timetable for the 1989 Awards required completed nominations to be submitted by September 8th 1989. Awards were presented on November 2nd in London.

Future: Firmly established as the 'flagship' of Whitbread's community involvement programme the Awards look certain to continue, under a different name, in the next few years.

Entry: On the official nomination form. No supporting material is permitted. Judging is based solely on written nominations.

WIMPY ENVIRONMENTAL AWARDS with UK 2000

UK 2000, Unit 101, Butlers Wharf Business Centre, 45 Curlew Street London SE1 2ND
Tel: 071 378 1847

Contact: Press Officer
Sponsor: Wimpy International Ltd

The scheme is for environmental projects and groups supported ('kitemarked') by UK 2000, or NI 2000 in Northern Ireland. The scheme, which was established in 1986, aims to stimulate good quality environmental project work with local involvement. In 1989 entries were required to demonstrate: environmental improvement, job enhancement and benefit to the community. The scheme has a regional component – offering awards of £500, £200 and £100 to the three best projects in five regions: Northern England, Southern England, Wales, Scotland and Northern Ireland. The three national winners, chosen from the regional finalists, were awarded £2000, £500 and £200 at a reception in October 1989. The scheme has an interesting feature in that (in the 1989 scheme) shortlisted entries were invited to free training seminars on presentational skills. These sessions were designed to help the projects improve their effectiveness in seeking publicity, sponsorship and community involvement.

The 1989 National winners were the Sheffield City Wildlife Project, the Crossgar Nature Centre in County Down, and the Milton Keynes based Community Recycling Opportunities Programme. Regional winners included two cycleway projects, a scheme which turned a waste tip into a park, a heritage centre, and a small woodlands management project. Regional winners attracted valuable publicity in local and regional newspapers.

Future: As at December 1989 the future of the scheme was uncertain because Wimpy International had pulled out of sponsorship and a new sponsor was being sought. In January 1990 it was announced that the UK 2000 operation would not be continuing in its present form of funding.

Entry: On the official entry form with supporting information. Projects must be 'kitemarked' by the UK 2000 network before being eligible to enter.

WIMPY WALKS AWARDS

Civic Trust, 17 Carlton House Terrace, London SW1Y 5AW
Telephone: 071 930 0914

Contact: Celia Clark
Sponsor: Wimpy International

Following the 1989 competition Wimpy International will no longer be involved and a new sponsor is being sought. Although there is some uncertainty about the continuation of the scheme, and if it does the form it will take, we thought it would be useful to include brief information on the 1989 competition.

The 1989 'Trailblazers' Awards were designed to encourage children of primary school age to study their local environment and then devise suitable walks and trails of the locality for both local people and visitors.

The winning entry would be produced professionally with help from a designer and children's writer. In addition the winning school received £300 and the children involved £100 in savings certificates. Up to twelve further prizes of £75 and a certificate of merit were also awarded.

The timetable for the 1989 competition required entries to be submitted by 1st May with results announced by the end of June.

Future: The future of the scheme is uncertain because of Wimpy's decision to withdraw from sponsorship.

YOUNG CONCERT ARTISTS' AWARD

National Federation of Music Societies, Francis House, Francis Street, London, SW1P 1DE

Telephone: 071 828 7320

Contact: Cameron Mowat, Awards Administrator
Sponsor: Esso UK PLC

The Young Concert Artists' Award is included in this book mainly because it can benefit music societies as well as individual musicians and singers. The Award is designed to assist young concert artists to obtain engagements at the beginning of their professional career. It is run annually on a four-yearly cycle – each year focussing in turn on the following musical areas: pianists; women's voices; strings, wind and brass; and men's voices. The 1990 Award is for strings/wind/brass, and (presumably) the 1991 award will be for men's voices.

The winner in 1989 was the pianist Andrew West who was offered thirty engagements with NFMS societies throughout Britain, a solo recital at the Purcell Room on London's South Bank, funds to commission a work from a composer, financial assistance towards a promotional brochure, and a cash prize of £100. Runners-up are offered solo recitals in Manchester and Glasgow and ten engagements each with NFMS Societies.

The benefit to NFMS member societies, the main interest here, lies in sponsorship (from Esso UK plc) which funds the cost of the engagement fee for the artists concerned, currently a standard £90, for concerts organised by societies. Thus a society can put on a high quality concert without having to find the cost of the performer's fee and with the publicity advantages associated with a 'national award winner'. Societies must cover hospitality and travel expenses but it may be possible for these to be shared with other societies if tours can be arranged.

Societies are invited to apply for concerts by the winners. The first thirty to do so are able to engage the winner and the next ten likewise for each runner-up. A 'waiting list' of unsuccessful applications is held. It is very clearly 'first come, first served'.

However specific dates and venues do not need to be confirmed with the initial application – all that was required in 1989 was that societies gave a commitment to stage an event before July 1990.

Future: A well established scheme which we assume will continue.

Entry: Application forms for individual artists and for societies wishing to bid for concerts are available from NFMS, in the case of the 1990 (strings/wind/brass) award, from January 1990.

YOUNG DEAF ACHIEVERS AWARD

Young Deaf Achievers Award, Deaf Accord, 311 Gray's Inn Road, London WC1X 8PT

Contact: Maggie Mooge, YDA Coordinator
Sponsor: British Telecom in 1989

This award scheme is designed to 'show that many deaf young people can rise to considerable achievement despite their disability..[and be]...an inspiration to others'. The awards are open to deaf, deaf-blind or hard of hearing people between the age of 16 and 29 who have 'achieved something exceptional in any field – career, sport, bravery, scholarship and so on'. Entry is through third party nomination and there are no restrictions on who may nominate an individual for an award.

The three winners in 1988 received awards, from the Princess of Wales, of £500, £300 and £200 together with an engraved glass memento. These were Matthew James for his academic career and adventurous travel programme, Alan Mather for academic and personal achievement and Angela Hill who now runs her own highly successful hairdressing business. The judging procedure involves the selection of regional 'finalists' who are invited to attend the Awards Luncheon. From these the three national winners are chosen.

The 1989 Awards' timetable required nominations to be submitted by 31st August 1989.

Future: Uncertain.

Entry: On the official nomination form.

YOUTH CLUBS OF THE YEAR

Youth Clubs UK, Keswick House, 30 Peacock Lane, Leicester, LE1 5NY
Telephone: 0533 29514

Sponsor: Encyclopaedia Britannica

This award scheme aims to achieve a greater recognition of the work with young people carried out by youth clubs, groups and projects throughout the country (the United Kingdom). The awards are made to clubs, groups and projects which impress the selection panel as having a relevant and effective activity or programme in a number of specific fields. In 1989 these were:

- Promoting health and fitness .... helping young people to make informed choices on health matters and promoting positive programmes for fitness and good physical, mental and spiritual health.

- Fostering creativity ....providing opportunities for young people to express themselves, their views and feelings creatively, and encouraging recognition and appreciation of creativity in others.

- **Coping with change** .... helping young people face difficult, unexpected or unwanted transitions in their lives, and helping them develop knowledge and skills to cope with the changes and choices.
- **Promoting social justice and equality** .... providing the means by which injustices and inequalities affecting young people can be addressed, both within and beyond the youth club movement.
- **Helping young people in trouble** .... supporting, helping, assisting and working with young people in trouble.
- **Community participation** .... providing opportunities for young people to develop the knowledge, skills and confidence to play a full and effective part in the world in which they live.

For each category there is one award of £750 and two of £250, which must be spent on developing the programme of activities or facilities of the clubs, groups or projects selected. A maximum of 60 entrants are shortlisted for an award and each receives a Britannica Atlas.

Youth Clubs UK produces the initial shortlist of 60 nominees who are then invited to submit further information. A panel appointed by Youth Clubs UK and including voluntary, part-time and full-time youth workers then makes the final selection. Winners in 1988 included groups in Goole, Rhondda, Aspatria, New Malden and West London.

For the 1989 competition nominations were due by 1st September 1989 and awards presented in February 1990.

Future: This scheme will continue, although the specific categories change from year to year.

Entry: Nominations, on the official form, may be made by 'anyone who is familiar with the work of the club/group/project' and may include participating young people, parents, community activists and youth officers.

INDEX (by subject)

The competitions and award schemes described in this book are, for the purposes of this index, listed under thirteen subject headings which reflect their main focus. In a few cases a scheme is listed under more than one heading but readers should note that many schemes have a breadth which their title belies. It should also be noted that several schemes are open to individuals as well as organisations. Only those which concentrate upon recognising individual as opposed to collective achievement are included in the 'individual achievement' category.

We have indicated the geographical eligibility of entrants or entered projects although we advise you to always check with organisers in case entry conditions have changed. A small number of schemes are open only to members of a particular organisation – these we have denoted with an R for 'restricted'.

UK – United Kingdom: Great Britain and Northern Ireland

GB – Great Britain: England, Scotland and Wales

BI – British Isles: UK, Eire, Shetlands, Isle of Man

		Page
ARTS		
ABSA/Daily Telegraph Awards	UK	9
Art and Work Awards	UK	11
Arts in the Community Awards	UK	12
BBC Choir Girl of the Year	UK	19
BET Choristers Awards	UK	28
The Daily Telegraph Award	UK	49
Prudential Awards for the Arts	UK	108
Sainsbury's Choir of the Year	UK	123
TSW Shootfirst Award	*TSW TV area*	144
Young Concert Artists Awards	*GB*	159
BUSINESS/INDUSTRY		
Business and Industry Environment Awards	UK	33
The Dragon Awards	*Companies with London base*	54
Livewire Awards	UK	95
Rural Employment Awards	*Rural England*	121

COMMUNITY PROJECTS/ORGANISATIONS

Community Partnership Prize	UK	42
Community Planning Awards	UK	43
Dulux Community Projects	UK	57
Ideas Annual Competition	UK	85
It's My City Awards	UK	87
Mersey Basin Campaign Awards	Mersey Basin	97
NFCO Publicity Competition	UK (R)	102
Times/RIBA Community Enterprise Scheme	UK	139
Twin Town Awards	UK	148
Village Hall Awards	Some English counties	149
Village Ventures Competitions	English/Welsh counties	150

COMMUNITY CARE/SOCIAL WELFARE

Community Care Enterprise Awards	UK	40
Co-operative Community Awards Scheme	UK	46
John Hunt Awards	England & Wales	90
Tunstall Telecom National Caring Awards	UK	146
Whitbread Volunteer Action Awards	UK	156

DISABILITY/HEALTH

AFASIC Christmas Card Competition	UK	10
Dista Awards	UK	51
Domestos Health Education Awards	UK	52
Independent Living Awards	Europe	86
Jaap Joustra Award	UK	89
Ratcliff Mobility Awards	UK	110
Young Deaf Achievers Awards	UK	160

EDUCATION/SCHOOLS

The Daily Telegraph School Newspaper Competition	UK	50
Education through Heritage & the Arts	UK	59
Environmental Enterprise Award	UK	62
Eyebright Junior	Strathclyde	69
North York Moors National Park Conservation Awards	NYM National Park	104

Royal Insurance Young Critics Awards	UK	114
Royal Mail Young Letter Writers Competition	UK	116
Wimpy Walks Awards	UK	158

ENVIRONMENT

APRS Awards	Scotland	16
Augustine Courtauld Awards	Essex	17
BBC Design Awards	UK	20
Best Kept Village Competitions	English/Welsh Counties	22
Brecknock Community Environmental Projects Competition	Brecknock District	30
Britain in Bloom	UK, Isle of Man & Jersey	31
Business and Industry Environment Awards	UK	33
Civic/Architectural Design Awards	various	37
Colonel Sanders Environment Awards	UK	39
Community Pride Awards	UK (R)	44
Countryside Caretakers Awards	Wales	47
Country Life Farming and Wildlife Awards	UK	48
Duchy of Cornwall Young Farmers' Clubs Countryside Projects Awards	UK (R)	55
(County) Durham Environment Awards	Durham County	58
Edward Morshead Award	Dartmoor National Park	60
Elmbridge Community Clean-Up Prize	Elmbridge Borough	61
Environmental Enterprise Awards	UK	62
Environment Week Awards	various localities	64
Ethnic Minorities Award Scheme	UK	65
Europa Nostra Awards	Europe	66
Eyebright	Scotland	68
Eyebright Junior	Scotland	69
Ford Conservation Awards	UK/Europe	70
Gloucestershire Footpath Heritage Competition	Gloucestershire	75
Graham Allen Award for Conservation	North Norfolk	76
Green Con of the Year Award	UK	78

Green Leaf Housing Awards	UK (R)	80
John Mejor Awards	Devon	92
Mersey Basin Campaign Awards	Mersey Basin	97
Norfolk Society Awards	Norfolk	103
Northumberland Tree and Hedgerow Cup	Northumberland	105
Pride of Place Awards	UK	106
Prince of Wales Awards	Wales	107
RICS Conservation Awards	UK	112
RSPB Birds and Countryside Awards	UK	120
Rural Wales Awards	UK	122
Shell Better Britain Campaign	UK	131
South Somerset Environment Awards Scheme	South Somerset	133
Tennent Community Award	Scotland	134
Theakston Heritage Fund	GB	135
The THF Community Chest	UK	137
The Times/PM Environment Awards	UK	138
Trees for People: Arboretum Competition	UK	143
Wimpy Environmental Awards	UK	157

HOUSING/PLANNING

Civic/Architectural Design Awards	various	37
Community Planning Awards	UK	43
Green Leaf Housing Award	UK (R)	80
Habitat Awards	International	82
RTPI Award for Planning Achievement	BI	118
Tomorrow's New Communities Competition	UK (projects)	141

INDIVIDUAL ACHIEVEMENT

Dista Awards	UK	51
Jaap Joustra Awards	UK	89
Lincoln Civic Award	Lincoln City	93
Mayor of Bournemouth Volunteer of the Year Award	Bournemouth	96
Midlands Women of the Year	East & West Midlands	98
Reform 'Compassionate Action' Trust Award	UK	111

Right Livelihood Awards	*International*	113
T.S.Shipman Prize	*Loughborough (R)*	144
Tunstall Telecom National Caring Awards	UK	146
Wainwright Achievement Award	*Kendal*	155
Whitbread Volunteer Action Awards	UK	156
Young Deaf Achievers Award	UK	160

MUSEUMS/HERITAGE/ARCHAEOLOGY

Association for Industrial Archaeology Awards	UK	14
Education through Heritage & the Arts	UK	59
Europa Nostra	*Europe*	66
Gateway Interpret Britain Award	UK *(& Shetlands, Orkneys, Channel Islands)*	72
Glenfiddich Living Scotland Awards	*Scotland*	74
Gulbenkian Museums and Galleries Awards	UK	81
Ian Allan Railway Heritage Awards	UK	84
Museum of the Year Awards	UK	99
Museum Year Award	UK	101
Sandford Award	UK	124
Scania/Transport Trust Awards	UK	126
Scottish Museum of the Year Awards	*Scotland*	127
Scottish Playground of the Year Awards	*Scotland*	128
Steam Heritage Awards	UK	134
Tennent Community Award	*Scotland*	134
VPB Design Award for Interpretive Panels	UK *(& Shetlands, Orkneys Channel Islands)*	154

TOURISM/RECREATION

Gloucestershire Footpath Heritage Competition	*Gloucestershire*	75
Scottish Tourism Award	*Scotland*	130
Wimpy Walks Awards	UK	158

VOLUNTARY SECTOR – GENERAL

BBC Design Awards	UK	20
Best Social Inventions Prize	UK	27
Caring in the Community	*Scotland*	34
Charity Annual Report and Accounts Awards	UK	35

Dragon Awards	*Companies with a London base*	54
Great Envelope Competition	UK	77
Ideas Annual Competition	UK	85
Literary Awards	*various*	94
Mayor of Bournemouth Volunteer of the Year (individual & group)	Bournemouth	96
Reform 'Compassionate Action' Trust Award	UK	111

YOUTH

Barclays Youth Action	UK	18
Best of British Youth Awards	UK	26
Youth Clubs of the Year Awards	UK	161